EASY SINGLE-POT PALEO COOKBOOK

Easy Paleo Meals for your busy COOKING:

150+ Healthy Recipes to cook

with minimal clan up!

By
Clarissa Williams

Introduction

Paleo diet is basically all about a version of a specific diet that aids in shedding weight and reducing various types of chronic conditions. This diet can also be termed as the caveman diet or Stone-Age diet. **The basic premise of this diet is to consume foods that can help an individual achieve optimum health.** This diet is based on the foods that were consumed mainly by the pre-historic Stone-Age people, so encourages the consumption of foods that are naturally grown and purely natural. Eating processed foods is absolutely forbidden in this diet: Paleo diet does not encourage the consumption of artificial additives, preservatives, sweeteners, coloring, artificial flavors, and chemical processes that are physically impossible to avoid. **All the ingredients used in this diet must be grown without using the aid of any chemical approaches.** Also, it is important to mention that this diet is strictly non-vegetarian and encourages the consumption of high fiber foods. The basic premise of this diet is completely on the replacement of processed foods with high fiber foods that are rich in soluble minerals and vitamins.

Why could the Paleo Diet be good for you? This diet is completely focused on natural food, so your organism will produce fewer toxins and work better. **Do you know anything that it is better than eating completely natural foods?** I think it isn't easy. Moreover, **the reduction of carbohydrates is a fundamental principle of Paleo Diet**, so it can help you in **weight loss**! Scientific Researches discovered that following a low-carbohydrate and high-protein diet is regarded as one of the best ways to prevent cardiovascular diseases by overcoming digestive problems and increasing metabolic rates and fat burning. For this reason, I think a diet like Paleo Diet can be entirely adopted by every person who wants to maintain high healthy level, especially after a stressfully situation as days of busy job or fasting too.

The Paleo diet is an entirely new form of a diet; it also includes the principles of Keto dieting, that is based on following the consumption of natural foods that are rich in vitamins and minerals. Following the Paleo diet is very simple, because it is based on the caveman food. You only need to follow the principle of eating vegetables considered in the diet and need to start with steamed vegetables and a source of fruits to eat. There is no limitation for the types of fruits to eat: you can use in your meals a lot of varieties of fruits which are rich in vitamins and minerals, including figs, pineapples, apples, blueberries, bananas and many others.

In this book, you will find a lot of information about what you can eat and avoid, and through the 250+ fantastic recipes, you can organize your cooking, even if you are very busy!

Let's read together!

What is the Paleo Diet?

1. What is the Paleo diet?

Paleo diet is an Asian caveman food that is completely based on natural food. It has been in practice for around 200,000 years. This diet is also known as the caveman diet or paleo diet. Hence as the name suggests, it strives to imitate the lifestyle of prehistoric times. One of the most notable things about this diet is that it is not linked to any religion; however, it is a non-vegetarian diet. This diet is completely based on the consumption of strictly natural foods. These foods are selected and grown without using any chemicals or the aid of fertilizers. These foods include; meat, fowl, fish, eggs and other vegetables. Thus, this diet is purely natural. Paleo diet is also known as the low-carb diet. This diet is completely non-vegetarian. It solely focuses on the consumption of meat, fish, fowl, shellfish, meats, eggs, nuts and seeds. This diet allows the consumption of a small amount of vegetables, fruits, and nuts. The major purpose behind the creation of this diet was to reduce the consumption of grains and processed foods. This concept was that grains and processed foods were not healthy. The carbohydrate-heavy diet also began to be termed as a "modern diet" by many. Hence the Paleo diet focused on the reduction of consumption of such carbohydrates.

2. How does Paleo diet Work?

Paleo diet is a completely natural approach to dieting, and it encourages the consumption of foods that are natural and in process foods. The basic working of this diet is simple. If one intakes food that are natural in nature, then the body becomes capable of burning excess fats and stores which are already present. This is all possible due to the fact that these natural foods are rich in fiber content. Hence, they act as a detoxifying agent for the body. They are capable of helping the body in fast means of shedding weight and thus reducing weight by means of increasing metabolic rates and productive functioning of the body. So essentially the Paleo diet is a natural approach and a healthier alternative to other diets and products.

3. Why Paleo Diet is good for you?

The fundamental essence of Paleo diet is completely natural, and it focuses on the consumption of natural foods. This diet focuses on fresh vegetables, fruits and other high fiber foods that are natural in nature. The Paleo diet is a completely vegetarian diet and also a diet which is completely devoid of any other additive. Thus, Paleo diet is somewhat similar to some extent to the concept of organic products and organic dieting. The idea behind the Paleo diet is to reduce the consumption of normal and processed foods. Thus, the Paleo diet is a brand of diet that has a target at maintaining a healthy body. carbohydrates that are not submissive to digestion and are processed foods are also forbidden in the Paleo diet.

The popularity of the Paleo diet is increasing tremendously every year and people are shifting towards this diet owing to its positive results. This is an example of an approach that is based on the natural way of life. As opposed to other types of diets, this kind of diet is completely based on natural food that is considered to be the best suited for human consumption. Paleo diet is especially considered to be a way of weight loss dieting. It is indeed a diet which is capable of preparing the body to shed excess weight and is also capable of removing the inflammation that is caused due to a number of reasons. All the components that are provided in the diet are essential in nature and therefore they assist in treating the nature caused issues. These components can be obtained from the consumption of meats, fish, vegetables, fruits, etc. It is a diet that is also capable of preventing the occurrence of health issues such as obesity, cardiovascular diseases, diabetes, etc. by increasing the metabolic rate and bodyweight more rapidly and more efficiently.

WHAT CAN YOU EAT IN PALEO DIET?

Following, there is a guideline about foods you can eat or not in Paleo diet. Practically you should eat only unprocessed food such as fresh meats, vegetables, and fruits.

However, each people can adapt Paleo diet in his/her lifestyle. I think each diet should be an instrument in our life to have healthier and more wellness, not a "dogma": so, I agree with a less rigid and more flexible Paleo diet, with some little "exception". Then, in this book, I wanted to insert some recipes with some more refined ingredients, bordering the Paleo diet, to allow people to start the Paleo diet gradually!

However, following there are some foods you can eat in Paleo Diet.

VEGETABLES

- Agretti
- Asparagus
- Basil
- Broccoli
- Artichokes
- Carrots
- Brussel Spout
- Cauliflower
- Cabbage
- Cucumbers
- Chicory
- Onions
- Mushrooms
- Salad
- Eggplant
- Radicchio
- Turnip
- Radish
- Shallot
- Celery
- Pumpkin
- Zucchini

FISH

- Anchovy
- Bleak
- Alice
- Lobster
- Herring
- Squid
- Scallops
- Capitone
- Carp
- Mullet
- Cicerello
- Mussel
- Mollusk
- Gallinella
- Snapper
- Shrimp
- Crab
- Halibut
- Cod
- Hake
- Moscardino
- Sea bream
- Oysters
- Palombo
- Perch
- Catfish
- Octopus
- Rhombus
- Salmon
- Sarago
- Sardine
- Sepia
- Emery
- Sole
- Sea bass
- Tuna
- Mullet
- Trout
- Clam

DRINKS

- Water
- Coconut water
- Smoothies
- Herbal tea

OILS AND FATS

- Coconut oil
- Ghee
- Duck fat
- Coconut milk
- Avocado oil
- Linseed oil
- Almond oil
- Hazelnut oil
- Walnut oil
- Red Palm oil
- Fish oil
- Pumpkin seed oil
- Bacon
- Lard

FRUIT

- Apricot
- Black cherry
- Pineapple
- Oranges
- Avocado
- Goji berries
- Bananas
- Cedar
- Cherries
- Coconut
- Watermelon
- Dates
- Kiwi
- Passion fruit
- Strawberries
- Lime
- Lemon
- Mango
- Apple
- Pomegranate
- Papaya
- Tamarind
- Currants
- Grapes

MILK

- Horchata
- Coconut milk
- Kefir milk
- Hazelnut milk
- Almond milk

EGGS

ALGAE

- Arame
- Clorella
- Agar Agar
- Klamath
- Spirulina

SEEDS AND NUTS

- Cashew
- Chestnuts
- Almonds
- Hazelnuts
- Walnuts
- Brazilian nuts
- Macadamia nuts
- Pecan nuts
- Pistachios
- Cocoa beans
- Carob seeds
- Sunflower seeds
- Flax seeds
- Poppy seeds
- Sesame seeds
- Pumpkin seeds
- Chia seeds

MEAT

- Lamb
- Duck
- Woodcock
- Bison
- Buffalo
- Capon
- Goat
- Roe deer
- Horse
- Rabbit
- Hen
- Hare
- Pig
- Beef
- Goose
- Pigeon
- Chicken
- Turkey
- Game

Animal Organs
(tongue, liver,
kidneys,

TUBERS AND ROOTS

- Beetroot
- Daikon
- Sweet Potatoes
- Topinambur
- Chufa
- Tigernut

DRINKS

- Water
- Coconut water
- Smoothies
- Herbal tea

FLOURS

- Banana flour
- Hemp flour
- Chestnut flour
- Chufa flour
- Coconut flour
- Almond flour
- Arrowroot
- Sweet Potato flour

Breakfast Recipes

1. Super Moroccan Lemon Beef Stew

Preparation Time: 20 minutes

Cooking Time: 4 hours

Servings: 4 to 6

Ingredients:

- 1 medium butternut squash (Diced)
- Pinch of salt and pepper, each
- 3 medium yellow onions (Diced)
- 1/3 cup butter
- 3 garlic cloves (Minced)
- Juice from 2 lemons
- 2 ½ tablespoons raselhanout spice
- 2 cups beef broth
- 2 pounds stewing beef

Directions:

1. Place all the ingredients but the squash in the slow cooker.
2. Cover and cook properly on medium for about 3 to 4 hours, until meat is tender.
3. Add the squash to the cooker; then cook properly for another hour.
4. Finally serve in bowls, over rice.

2. Reliable Blueberry and Dates- Breakfast cereal

Preparation Time: 20 to 30 Minutes

Cooking Time: 30 to 40 Minutes

Servings: 4 to 6

Ingredients:

- ½ cup unsweetened coconut flakes
- 1 tsp. sea salt
- 1 cup pumpkin seeds
- 1 tablespoon vanilla
- 2 cups almond flour
- 2 ½ teaspoons Cinnamon
- 6 medium dates, pitted
- 1/3 cup coconut oil
- ½ cup dried blueberries

Directions:

1. Preheat your oven to about 310 to 320°F.
2. Add coconut oil, dates and half the almond flour to a food processor and mix it thoroughly. Add pumpkin seeds and continue pulsing until roughly chopped. Next, transfer the mixture to a large bowl and add cinnamon, vanilla and salt; spread on a baking sheet and bake for about 20 to 25 minutes or until browned.
3. Finally remove from the oven and let cool slightly before stirring in blueberries and coconut.

3. Lucky Berry omelet

Preparation Time: 20 minutes

Cooking Time: 20 minutes

Servings: 2 to 3

Ingredients:

- 50g blueberries
- Bunch mint leaves
- About 55g blackberries
- 2 tablespoons coconut oil
- 50g raspberries
- 4 eggs

Directions:

1. Pre-heat a frying pan over medium heat, pour 1 tablespoon coconut oil.
2. Whisk eggs in the bowl, transfer half of them to the pan. Cook properly for about 2 to 5 minutes. Add half of the berries and fold the omelet to cover the berries and cook properly for about 2 more minute. Finally remove to a plate and repeat the process with the remaining ingredients.

4. Charming Lemon Thyme Lamb Chops

Preparation Time: 20 to 25 minutes
Cooking Time: 10 to 15 minutes
Servings: 2 to 4
Ingredients:

- Sea salt
- Lemon juice – 1
- Olive oil about 1/4 cup
- Fresh thyme
- Lamb chops – 4

Directions:

1. In a large dish, place the lamb chops then cover with lemon juice, oil and thyme leaves.
2. Cover the mixture and let sit at room temperature for about 20 minutes. Turn the chops to marinate evenly.
3. Apart from, preheated a pan; lower the heat and grill the chops for about 2 to 5 minutes per side. Grill the lemons with the chops.
4. Finally serve immediately then sprinkle with fresh thyme leaves and sea salt.

5. Energetic Baked Salmon with Lemon and Thyme

Preparation Time: 10 minutes
Cooking Time: 25 minutes
Servings: 4 to 6
Ingredients:

- About 1.5 lemon, sliced thin
- Olive oil, for drizzling
- About 1.5 tbsp. capers
- 1 tbsp. fresh thyme
- Salt and freshly ground pepper
- 32 oozes piece of salmon

Directions:

1. Line a rimmed baking sheet with parchment paper and then place salmon, skin side down, on the prepared baking sheet; then generously season salmon with salt and pepper. Arrange capers on the salmon, and top with sliced lemon and thyme. Place baking sheet in a cold oven, then turn heat to 400° F.
2. Finally bake for about 20 to 25 minutes. Serve immediately.

6. Funny Sautéed Kale

Preparation Time: 15 to 20 Minutes   **Cooking Time:** 15 to 20 Minutes

Servings: 2 to 3

Ingredients:

- 2 tablespoons sliced almonds
- A pinch of sea salt to taste
- 1/4 onion (Diced)
- 1 ½ tablespoon extra-virgin olive oil
- 2 garlic cloves (Minced)
- 4 cups rinsed and chopped kale

Directions:

1. First of all, quickly heat extra virgin olive oil in a medium skillet set over medium heat; add onion and saute for about 5 to 10 minutes or until translucent.
2. Add garlic, kale and almonds and cook properly for about 5 to 10 minutes or until kale is tender. Finally season with sea salt to serve.

7. Delightful Double chocolate cookies

Preparation Time: 10 minutes
Cooking Time: 20 minutes
Servings: 24 to 26 cookies
Ingredients:

- 1 cup cocoa powder
- 1 pinch sea salt
- 1 egg
- 1 cup almond butter
- 1 tbsp coconut oil
- 50 g of crumbled walnuts

Directions:

1. Preheat oven to about 340 to 350° F.
2. Mix all the ingredients in a bowl. Next, line a large baking sheet with parchment paper.
3. Finally form the cookies with a tablespoon and bake them for about 10 to 15 minutes, until just cooked.

8. Fantastic Gingersnaps

Preparation Time: 15 minutes
Cooking Time: 15 to 20 minutes
Servings: 24 to 26 cookies
Ingredients:

- 1 egg
- 1 pinch of sea salt
- About 2.5 tbsps. raw honey
- ¼ tsp freshly ground nutmeg
- 2 teaspoons powdered ginger
- About ½ tsp ground cloves
- 1 tsp cinnamon

- 1 cup almond butter

Directions:

1. Preheat oven to about 340 to 350 °F.
2. Mix all the ingredients in a bowl; then quickly line a large baking sheet with a parchment paper.

3. Finally form the cookies with a tablespoon and bake them for about 10 to 15 minutes, until just cooked.

9. Great Garlic mushrooms with bacon

Preparation Time: 10 minutes
Cooking Time: 15 to 20 minutes
Servings: 2 to 3 portions
Ingredients:

- 3 bacon rashers
- Pinch salt and pepper
- 3 garlic cloves
- 2 ½ tablespoons chopped parsley
- 3 tablespoons olive oil
- 210g Portobello mushrooms

Directions:

1. Pre-heat a grill pan over medium-high heat, pour olive oil.
2. Apart from, wash mushrooms, dry them with paper towels, slice. Dice bacon rashers, chop garlic cloves and mix them with sliced mushrooms in a bowl. Put all the ingredients in the grill pan. Fry for about 5 to 10 minutes, stirring from time to time.
3. Finally transfer to the plates, add salt and pepper, decorate with chopped parsley.

10. Happy Delicious Glazed Carrots

Preparation Time: 10 to 15 minutes
Cooking Time: 3 to 4 hours
Servings: 8 to 9
Ingredients:

- 3/4 cup of water
- A pinch of nutmeg, ground
- ½ cup raw honey
- 1 teaspoon cinnamon, ground
- A pinch of sea salt
- 2 pounds carrots (Sliced)

Directions:

1. Put carrots in your slow cooker.
2. Add water, salt, raw honey, cinnamon and nutmeg, toss well, cover and cook properly on high heat for about 2 to 3 hours.
3. Finally stir again, divide between plates and serve as a side dish.

11. Lucky Quinoa Veggie Breakfast Bowl

Preparation Time: 15 minutes
Cooking Time: 20 minutes
Servings: 3
Ingredients:

- Salt and pepper
- ½ cup of water
- ½ cup broccoli (Chopped)
- ½ cup of Coconut milk
- ½ cup of sliced mushrooms
- 1 egg
- ½ cup quinoa, rinsed

Directions:

1. Add olive oil to a skillet set over medium heat. Add mushrooms and broccoli and stir-fry for about 5 to 10 minutes or until cooked through. Remove the skillet from heat and set aside.
2. In a saucepan, combine water, quinoa, and coconut milk; bring to a gentle boil and lower heat to low. Then simmer until almost all liquid is absorbed.
3. Stir in veggies, cheese, and salt and pepper until well combined. Cover and set aside.

4. Fry the egg sunny side up. Finally serve quinoa in a bowl topped with the egg.

12. Vintage Zucchini and Sweet Potato (Fritatta)

Preparation Time: 5 to 10 minutes
Cooking Time: 20 to 25 minutes
Servings: 2 to 4
Ingredients:

- Fresh parsley – 1 tablespoon
- Pepper and salt to taste
- Eggs – 8
- 1 cutted, peeled large sweet potato
- Red bell pepper – 1 (Sliced)
- Sliced zucchini – 2
- 2 ½ tablespoons Butter or coconut oil

Directions:

1. Add oil to a cooking pan then heat over medium heat, then add the slices of sweet potato and cook properly for about 5 to 10 minutes. Add red bell pepper and zucchini slices.
2. Continue cooking for about 2 to 5 minutes. While still cooking, whisk the eggs into a bowl.
3. Season the egg with pepper and salt; add to the vegetables.
4. Cook properly over low heat for about 10 to 15 minutes then in a heated broiler allow the frittata to become golden.
5. Finally cut the frittata into pieces then have it served with fresh parsley.

13. Best Butternut Squash and Kale Beef Stew

Preparation Time: 35 minutes
Cooking Time: 55 minutes
Servings: 8 to 10
Ingredients:

- 2 lb. stew beef, 1" cubed
- Salt and pepper
- 1 onion, roughly chopped
- 4 cups beef stock,
- 4 garlic cloves (Minced)
- 16oz frozen, chopped kale
- 1 ½ tablespoon fresh sage (Minced)
- ½ tsp paprika
- 4 cups butternut squash, cubed
- 2 ½ tablespoons bacon fat

Directions:

1. In a slow cook quickly heat 1 tbsp. bacon fat over medium high; then working in batches, brown the meat, making sure not to cook it properly through (it can turn tough). Set browned meat aside. Lower heat to medium and add the 2nd tbsp. bacon fat.
2. Once it's melted add the garlic, onions, smoked paprika, and sage to pot, along with a big pinch of salt and fresh pepper. Cook properly about 5 to 10 minutes, or until the onions begin to soften and turn translucent. Then make sure to stir frequently so the mixture doesn't burn.
3. Add the beef, butternut squash, and kale to the pot. Stir to combine. Add the chicken stock and 2 cups of hot water. Bring to a boil, then reduce to a simmer and let cook, covered, for at least an hour. If it needs, let it stand about 40 to 45 minutes longer.

Lunch Recipes

14. Spicy Turkey Chili

Cooking Time: 15 minutes
Preparation Time: 3 hours 45 minutes
Servings: 6
Ingredients:

- 2 pounds boneless, cutted turkey thighs
- 1 yellow onion
- 3 chopped garlic cloves
- 2 jalapeno pepper, seeded
- 2 tablespoons chili powder
- 1 can chiles
- 2 larghe tomatoes
- 15 ounces black beans, drained
- 1 tablespoon white vinegar
- Salt and pepper to taste
- Minced cilantro for serving

Directions:

1. Fill a pot with 3/4 of water. Add in chopped turkey, chopped onion, garlic, chopped jalapeño, chopped tomatoes, chili powder. Season with salt and pepper. Cover with the lid and cook on medium for 3 hours. Add beans and cook for another 30 minutes, then stir in vinegar and cook for another 10 minutes. Serve with sliced cilantro.

15. Super Paleo Mexican Beef Stew

Preparation Time: 25 minutes
Cooking Time: 6 hours 5 minutes
Servings: 2
Ingredients:

- 1 garlic clove (Minced)
- Pinch of salt and fresh ground pepper
- About 1 red onion (Chopped)
- 2 cups of water
- 4 ounces green chilies (Diced)
- 3 large tomatoes (Chopped)
- 1 teaspoon cumin
- About 1.5 teaspoon oregano
- 2 teaspoons chili powder
- 1-pound stewing beef
- 2 cups beef broth

Directions:

1. Slice the stewing beef into thin slices. Place all the ingredients in your pot.
2. Cover and cook properly on low for about 4 to 5 hours. Finally serve in bowls.

16. Beef Broth

Cooking Time: 6 hours 45 minutes
Preparation Time: 6 hour 45 minutes
Servings: 4
Ingredients:

- 5 pounds beef meets
- 1 pound of stew meat cutted
- Olive oil
- 1-2 onions, chopped
- 2 large carrots, chopped
- 1 celery rib, chopped
- 2 cloves of garlic
- Handful of parsley
- 1-2 bay leaves
- 10 peppercorns

Directions:

1. Heat oven to 375°F. Rub olive oil over the stew meat pieces, carrots, and onions. Place stew meat or beef scraps, stock bones, carrots and onions in a large roasting pan. Roast in oven for about 45 minutes, turning everything half-way through the cooking. Place everything from the oven in the

slow cooker and cook on low for 6 hours. After cooking, remove the bones and vegetables from the pot. Strain the broth. Let cool to room temperature and then put in the refrigerator. The fat will solidify once the broth has chilled. Discard the fat (or reuse it) and pour the broth into a jar and freeze it.

17. Chicken Broth Ingredients

Preparation Time: 6 hours

Cooking Time: 6 hours

Servings: 6

Ingredients:

- 4 lbs. fresh whole chicken
- 2 peeled onions
- 2 celery stalks
- 1 carrot
- 8 black peppercorns
- 2 sprigs fresh thyme
- 2 sprigs fresh parsley
- 1 teaspoon salt

Directions:

Put all ingredients in your pot and cook on low for 6 hours. Let cool to warm room temperature and strain. Keep chilled and use or freeze broth within a few days.

18. Lentil Soup

Preparation Time: 4 hours

Cooking Time: 4 hours

Servings: 6

Ingredients

- 2 tablespoons olive oil
- 1 cup chopped onion
- ½ chopped carrot
- ½ chopped celery
- 2 teaspoons salt
- pound lentils
- 3 chopped tomatoes
- 2 cups vegetable broth
- ½ teaspoon coriander
- ½ teaspoon cumin

Instructions

Put all ingredients in the slow cooker and cook on low for 4 hours.

19. Black Bean Soup

Cooking Time: 8 hours

Servings: 6

Ingredients

- 14 tablespoons cup oil
- 1/2 Onion, Diced
- 1/4 cup Carrots, Diced
- 1/2 Green Bell Pepper, Diced
- 1 cup beef broth
- 2 pounds raw Black Beans
- 1 tablespoon lemon juice
- 1/2 Garlic clove
- Salt and pepper to taste
- 2 teaspoons Chili Powder
- 8-pounds pork meat
- 1 tablespoon flour
- 1/2 cup water

Instructions

Put all ingredients in slow cooker and cook on low for 8 hours.

20. Squash soup

Servings: 6

Cooking Time: 4 hours

Ingredients

- 1 Squash, seeds removed, chopped
- 1 carrot, chopped
- 1 onion (diced)

13

- 1 cup coconut milk
- 1/2 cup water
- 2 tablespoons Olive oil
- Salt and pepper to taste
- 2 teaspoons cinnamon
- 2 teaspoons turmeric

Instructions

Put all ingredients in the slow cooker and cook on low for 4 hours. Blend until smooth and creamy. Sprinkle it with toasted pumpkin seeds

21. Greek lemon chicken soup

Servings: 4
Cooking Time: 4 hours
Ingredients:

- 4 cups chicken broth
- 1/4 cup uncooked brown rice
- Salt and pepper to taste
- 3 eggs
- 3 tablespoons lemon juice
- Handful fresh dill (chopped)
- Shredded roasted chicken

Directions:

1. In a bowl whisk lemon juice and the eggs until smooth. Add about 1 cup of the hot broth into the egg/lemon mixture and whisk to combine.
2. Put all ingredients in the slow cooker and cook on low for 4 hours.

22. Fantastic Nori salmon handroll

Preparation Time: 10 minutes
Cooking Time: 15 minutes
Servings: 3
Ingredients:

- 1 green onion
- 1 toasted nori sheet
- 2 cucumbers
- 1/4 avocado
- 2 ½ ounces wild canned salmon

Directions:

1. First of all, slice avocado and cucumber and finely chop green onion.
2. Next, put the nori paper on a cutting board, layer the avocado, fish, 2 slices of cucumber and green onion. Finally wrap the paper around. Serve.

23. Great Amazing Eggplant Dip

Preparation Time: 15 minutes
Cooking Time: 4 hours and 10 to 15 minutes
Servings: 6
Ingredients:

- 1 zucchini (Chopped)
- Salt and pepper to taste
- 2 ½ tablespoons olive oil
- 2 tablespoons balsamic vinegar
- 1 ½ teaspoons garlic, minced
- 1 tablespoon parsley, chopped
- 1 yellow onion, chopped
- 3 tablespoons tomato paste
- 1 celery stick, chopped
- 1 tomato, chopped
- 1 eggplant

Directions:

1. First of all, brush eggplant with half of the oil, place them on a pan and cook properly over medium high heat for about 5 to 8 minutes on each side. Then quickly leave aside to cool down and then chop it. Grease your slow cooker with the rest of the oil and add eggplant pieces.

2. Add, onion, zucchini, vinegar, parsley, celery, tomato, tomato paste, salt and garlic, pepper and stir everything. Cover and cook properly on low heat for about 3 to 4 hours. Stir frequently.
3. Finally stir your spread again very well, divide into bowls and serve.

24. Happy Chicken, Leek and Asparagus Dill Casserole

Preparation Time: 15 Minutes
Cooking Time: 45 Minutes
Servings: 2
Ingredients:

- 250g Minced Chicken
- Sea salt and pepper
- 1/4 cup coconut milk
- ½ tsp. garlic powder
- 4 free range eggs, beaten
- 1 thinly sliced leek
- ½ tbsp. minced fresh dill
- 4 stalks asparagus, chopped
- Coconut oil, for greasing

Directions:

1. Preheat your oven to 320°F. Grease a square baking dish and set aside.
2. Place the chicken mince in a pan set over medium heat; break them into small pieces.
3. Cook for a few minutes and add asparagus and leeks; continue cooking for about 5 to 8 minutes more or maybe until chicken is no longer pink. Next, remove the pan from heat, discarding excess fat.
4. Finally whisk together eggs, coconut milk, garlic powder, dill, salt and pepper in a bowl; pour the mixture into the prepared baking dish and then quickly add the chicken mixture; mix well and then bake for about 45 to 48 minutes or maybe until set in the center.

25. Lucky Curried Chicken Salad

Preparation Time: 15 minutes
Cooking Time: 2 hours
Servings: 4
Ingredients:

- Cubed cooked chicken – 1 pound
- Fresh chives (Optional)
- Chopped jicama – 1/2 cup
- Small papayas, peeled and sliced in half
- Thinly sliced celery – 1 cup
- Mayonnaise – 1/4 cup
- Red curry paste – about 1.5 teaspoon
- Lemon flavor yogurt – 1/4 cup
- Soy sauce – about 2.5 teaspoons
- Orange – 1

Directions:

1. Peel orange, then segment into half or quarter. Place chicken, orange, grapes, jicama and celery in a bowl and combine.
2. For dressing use a small mixing bowl to combine mayonnaise, soy sauce, yogurt, and curry paste together.
3. Pour the dressing over the chicken mixture then toss lightly so as to coat. Cover the mixture

and allow to chill for a period of 1 hour or more. Finally serve in papaya halves or garnish with fresh chives.

26. Veggie Minestrone

Servings: 8
Cooking Time: 4 hours
Preparation Time: 4 hours 30 minutes
Ingredients

- 3 tablespoons olive oil
- 3 garlic cloves, chopped
- 1 onion, chopped
- 2 cups chopped celery
- 4 carrots, sliced
- 2 cups chicken broth
- 2 cups water
- 3 cups tomato sauce
- 1/2 cup red wine
- 1 cup raw kidney beans
- 1 cups green beans
- 2 cups baby spinach, rinsed
- 2 zucchinis, quartered and sliced
- 1 tablespoon chopped oregano
- 2 tablespoons chopped basil
- Salt and pepper to taste

Instructions

Put all ingredients in the slow cooker and cook on low for 4 hours.

27. Vegetarian Chili

Servings: 6
Cooking Time: 5 hours
Ingredients

- 1 tablespoon olive oil
- 1 cup chopped onions
- ½ cup chopped carrots
- 2 garlic cloves, minced
- ½ chopped green bell pepper
- ½ chopped red bell pepper
- ½ cup chopped celery
- 1 tablespoons chili powder
- 1 cup chopped mushrooms
- 3 cups chopped tomatoes
- 2 cups raw kidney beans
- 1 tablespoons ground cumin
- ½ teaspoon oregano
- ½ teaspoon minced basil leaves

Instructions

Put all ingredients in the slow cooker and cook on low for 5 hours.

28. Barbecued Beef

Servings: 8
Ingredients
Cooking Time: 4 hours

- ½ cups tomato paste
- 2 tablespoons lemon juice
- 2 tablespoons mustard
- Salt and pepper to taste
- ½ garlic clove
- 4 pounds boneless chuck roast

Instructions

Place chuck roast in a slow cooker. Pour all ingredients over and mix well. Cover, and cook on low for 4 hours.

29. Superfoods Chili

Servings: 6   **Cooking Time:** 4 hours   **Ingredients**

- 2 tablespoons olive oil
- 2 onions, chopped
- 3 garlic cloves, minced
- pound ground beef
- 2 cups beef sirloin, cubed
- 2 cups diced tomatoes

- 1 cup strong brewed coffee
- 1 cup tomato paste
- 2 cups beef broth
- 1 tablespoons cumin seeds
- 1 tablespoon cocoa powder
- 1 teaspoon ground coriander
- Salt and pepper to taste
- 6 cups cooked kidney beans
- 4 fresh hot chili peppers, chopped

Instructions

Put all ingredients in the slow cooker and cook on low for 4 hours.

30. Delicious Goulash

Servings: 6

Cooking Time: 4 hours

Ingredients

- 3 cups cauliflower
- 2 pounds ground beef
- 1 red onion, chopped
- Salt and pepper to taste
- 1 garlic clove
- 2 cups cooked kidney beans
- 1 cup tomato paste

Directions:

Put all ingredients in the slow cooker and cook on low for 4 hours.

31. Cabbage Stewed with Meat

Servings: 8

Cooking Time: 4 hours

Ingredients

- 2 pounds ground beef
- 1 cup beef stock
- 1 chopped red onion
- 1 bay leaf
- salt and pepper to taste
- 2 sliced celery ribs
- 4 cups shredded cabbage
- 1 carrot, sliced
- 1 cup tomato paste

Instructions

Put all ingredients in the slow cooker and cook on low for 4 hours.

32. Beef Stew with Peas and Carrots

Servings: 8

Cooking Time: 6 hours

Ingredients

- 3 large chopped carrots
- 1 large chopped onion
- 2 tablespoons olive oil
- 1 garlic clove minced
- 2 cups green peas
- 4 cups beef stock
- Salt and pepper to taste
- 4 pounds boneless chuck roast

Instructions

Put all ingredients in the slow cooker and cook on low for 6 hours.

33. Vintage Coconut Chicken w/ Mustard- Honey Sauce

Preparation Time: 20 to 25 Minutes

Cooking Time: 15 to 20 Minutes

Servings: 2 to 3

Ingredients:

- 1 cup unsweetened coconut flakes
- 1 cup steamed vegetables for serving
- 2 free range eggs
- 1/2 cup honey
- About 1 cup coconut flour
- 1/2 cup Dijon mustard
- 2 pounds boneless chicken breasts

Directions:

1. Preheat your oven to 400°F and line baking sheet with parchment paper. Then rinse the chicken and slice into small strips; pat them dry and set aside. Place coconut flour onto a plate and set aside. In a bowl, whisk the eggs and set aside. Place coconut flakes in another plate and set aside. Dip the chicken strips into the coconut flour, then into the eggs and finally into coconut flakes; arrange them onto the prepared baking sheet and bake for about 15 to 20 minutes or until browned.

2. Finally, meanwhile, combine honey and mustard in a bowl; drizzle over the baked chicken strips and serve with steamed veggies.

34. Green Beans and Almonds

Preparation Time: 10 minutes
Cooking Time: 15 minutes
Servings: 4
Ingredients:

- 1 lb green beans, trimmed
- 2 tbsps. butter
- ¼ cup sliced almonds
- 2 tsps. lemon pepper

Directions:

1. Steam the green beans for 8 minutes, until tender, then drain. On a medium heat, melt the butter in a skillet. Sauté the almonds until browned. Sprinkle with salt and pepper. Mix in the green beans. Serve.

35. Excellent Warrior Omelet

Preparation Time: 5 minutes   **Cooking Time:** 10 minutes   **Servings:** 2

Ingredients:

- 1 tablespoon olive oil
- ½ fresh avocado sliced into
- 1 green onions (Diced)
- 2 small tomatoes
- 1 cup fresh spinach leaves
- 2 eggs, scrambled

Directions:

1. Heat olive oil on low in nonstick omelet pan. Saute onions until tender. Add eggs and cook properly on low for about 2 to 5 minutes.
2. Add remaining ingredients, chopped. Finally, fold and flip omelet until eggs are fully cooked.

Dinner Recipes

36. Quick Eggs Benedict on Artichoke Hearts

Preparation Time: 20 minutes
Cooking Time: 1 hours 10 minutes
Servings: 1 to 2
Ingredients:

- Salt and pepper to taste
- As much turkey breasts, chopped
- ½ cup balsamic vinegar
- 2 cups artichoke hearts
- 2 eggs
- Hollandaise sauce
- 1 cup melted ghee
- 3 egg yolks
- Pinch of paprika
- 3/4 tablespoon lemon juice
- Pinch of salt
- 1 egg white

Directions:

1. First of all, line baking sheet with foil and preheat oven to 370° F.
2. Remove artichoke hearts from their dressing and place them in the balsamic vinegar for at least 15 to 20 minutes (but do not go over 30).
3. Fill a pot of water and simmer it on your stove for the Hollandaise sauce.
4. Melt the ghee (or butter) in a separate saucepan.
5. Separate your eggs, placing the yolks in a cooking bowl and hang on to the egg whites.
6. Take the artichoke hearts out of the marinade and then place them on the foil-lined sheet.
7. Brush them with the egg white before placing the turkey breasts over the artichokes' tops in a layer-like fashion. Put the tray in the oven for about 20 to 28 minutes.
8. Whisk the egg yolks in the lemon juice, then place the bowl (preferably stainless steel) over the pot of simmering water. This should create a double boiler.
9. Then, slowly add the ghee (or butter) and a little bit of salt.
10. Whisk it until it doubles in size and looks silky, then set aside.
11. Turn up the heat on the pot of water and get it boiling.
12. Crack the eggs in one at a time into a ladle, and then slide that spoon full of egg into the water. This will poach the eggs that go on top of the turkey breasts.
13. Let them sit in the water for 2 minutes, and then remove.
14. Take out the artichoke hearts and turkey breasts (if not already out) and lay them on a plate.
15. Finally place the poached egg on top and pour the Hollandaise sauce on top.
16. Sprinkle with salt, pepper, and paprika to taste. Enjoy!

37. Wonderful Paleo Crock Pot Chicken Soup

Preparation Time: 40 minutes   **Cooking Time:** 6 hours 10 minutes   **Servings:** 5
Ingredients:

- 4 cups filtered water
- 3 carrots, diced
- 3 celery stalks, diced
- Salt and pepper
- 1 tablespoon herbs de Provence
- 2 chicken thighs, with bone
- 2 chicken breasts, with bone, with skin

- 1 ½ teaspoon apple cider vinegar
- 1 medium onion, diced

Directions:

1. Place all the ingredients in a pot (or in a crock pot, if you have), ensuring the chicken is placed on top of the vegetables, bone should be side down. Add 4 cups of water, to cover the ingredients. Cook properly on low for about 5 to 6 hours, until meat flakes off bone and vegetables are fork tender. Once cooked, take out the chicken. Remove skin and bones.
2. Shred the chicken with 2 forks. Return pieces to the soup. Stir well. Taste. Season if needed.
3. Finally serve in bowls.

38. Tasty Paleo Delicious Zucchini Smoothie

Preparation Time: 5 to 10 Minutes
Cooking Time: 15 minutes
Servings: 2 to 4
Ingredients:

- 2 Cups of water
- 2.5 tbsps. Coconut Oil
- 1 Large Zucchini

- 1 Brown Onion

Directions:

1. First of all, rinse and pat dry and cut the Zucchini into slices. Chop the onion.
2. Heat the coconut oil in a pan under moderate heat and fry the onions until golden brown.
3. Add the Zucchini and cook properly under medium heat until tender.
4. Add 2 cups of water and boil. When boiling blend together.
5. Finally add a dash of salt to taste. Enjoy!

39. Iconic Italian Pulled Pork Ragu

Preparation Time: 5 Minutes
Cooking Time: 30 minutes
Servings: 2 to 4
Ingredients:

- 2 tablespoons minced parsley, divided
- Salt and pepper, to taste
- 2 bay leaves
- 1 teaspoon olive oil
- 4 garlic cloves, smashed with knife
- 2 sprigs fresh thyme
- 4 cups of finely chopped tomatoes
- 7 ounce roasted red peppers, drained
- 18 ounces pork tenderloin

Directions:

1. First of all, sprinkle the pork tenderloin with salt and pepper. Smash garlic cloves with the side of a knife. Finely chop tomatoes. Add oil to a preheated large pot (or Dutch oven if you have).
2. Add garlic and sauté over medium-high heat for about 2 minutes, until golden; then remove the garlic with a slotted spoon and set aside. Add pork and brown it on each side for about 2 to 5 minutes. Add tomatoes, fresh thyme, red peppers, bay leave and half of the chopped parsley.

3. Bring to a boil, cover, and cook properly on low heat for about 2.5 hours, until the fork is fork tender. Remove bay leaves and then shred the pork with 2 forks; serve over pasta topped with the remaining parsley.

40. Super Paleo One Pot Fajita Soup

Preparation Time: 15 Minutes
Cooking Time: 3 hours
Servings: 4
Ingredients:

- 1 yellow bell pepper (Diced)
- Juice from 1 lime
- 1 red bell pepper (Diced)
- 1 medium onion (Diced)
- 1.5 teaspoon ground pepper
- 1 teaspoon cumin
- 2 garlic cloves (Diced)
- 1 cup salsa
- About 1.5 teaspoon sea salt
- 1 green pepper (Diced)
- 4 cups chicken broth
- 1/2 jalapeño pepper, diced
- 1 Tablespoon chili powder
- 1 teaspoon paprika
- 2 pounds chicken, boneless, skinless
- 1 teaspoon olive oil
- Garnish: sour cream, cilantro

Directions:

1. Rinse the chicken, pat dry. Dice into cubes. Place the ingredients in your pot starting with the salsa then vegetables, and jalapeno. Add the chicken. Add the seasoning. Pour in the chicken broth. Cover and cook properly on low heat for about 3 hours. Test the chicken doneness. Cook longer if needed. Finally serve in bowls. Garnish with sour cream and cilantro.

41. Delightful Almond Butter Cups

Preparation Time: 10 Minutes
Cooking Time: 50 minutes
Servings: 1 dozen
Ingredients:
BASE:

- 2 tbsps. coconut butter
- Pinch of sea salt
- About 1.5 tsp pure maple syrup
- Pinch of cinnamon
- About 1/2 tsp pure vanilla extract
- 2 tbsps. coconut oil, melted
- 1/4 cup unsweetened cocoa powder

FOR THE FILLING:

- 1 tbsp coconut oil
- 1 pinch of sea salt
- About 1.5 tsp pure maple syrup
- 3 tbsps. almond butter

Directions:

1. First of all, whisk all the ingredients for the base in a mixing bowl. Put paper liners in a muffin baking tin, and spoon 1 teaspoon in each tin. Put in the fridge or freezer to set.
2. Mix all the ingredients for the filling and place in a pastry bag. Next, cut off a tiny corner of the bag with scissors. Take the cups from the fridge or freezer and add about 1/2 of the filling into the center of each cup, please cover with the base and then put back in the fringe or freezer.
3. Finally serve cold or at room temperature.

42. King sized Paleo Orange Chicken

Preparation Time: 15 minutes   **Cooking Time:** 15 minutes   **Servings:** 2

Ingredients:

- Salt and pepper
- Chicken thighs– 1 lb
- 4 tbsps. bacon fat

SAUCE:

- Orange juice – ½ cup
- Arrow root flour – 2 tbsps.
- Zest of large orange – 1
- Raw honey – 3 tbsps.
- Dash of red pepper flakes
- Coconut aminos – 3.5 tbsps.
- Water – 1 cup
- Ground ginger – ½

Directions:

1. First of all, season the chicken with pepper and sea salt, then set aside.
2. For the sauce, mix the ingredients in a saucepan and stir to combine.
3. Place the mixture over medium heat as you stir frequently. Allow the sauce to thicken and remove from heat. Heat bacon fat in a large skillet. Add the chicken, let it cook properly for about 5 to 10 minutes until browned. Drain excess fat from the pan and pour a portion of the sauce into the pan. Stir to coat the chicken. Remove from the heat and serve.
4. Finally pour the remaining portion of the sauce over some side steamed vegetables.

43. Yummy Kale Omelets

Preparation Time: 2 to 5 minutes

Servings: 1 to 3

Ingredients:

- Salt and pepper
- Chopped kale – 1 cup

Cooking Time: 5 to 10 minutes

- ½ tablespoon chopped chives
- Eggs – 3
- Butter – 1 tablespoon

Directions:

1.First of all, place a frying pan over medium heat then add butter and heat. Add kale to the pan then cook properly for about 5 to 10 minutes or until soft.

2.Beat the eggs in a bowl then add fresh chives, pepper and salt. Add egg mixture to the frying pan then swirl the pan for the mixture to spread to the edges. Cook properly on low heat until well set at the top. Finally fold over and serve.

44. Roasted Cabbage with Lime and Sriracha

Preparation Time: 25 minutes

Cooking Time: 45 minutes

Servings: 2

Ingredients:

- 2 tablespoons avocado oil
- 2 teaspoons sesame seeds
- 2 tablespoons lime juice
- 1/2 teaspoon sea salt
- 2.5 teaspoons Sriracha sauce
- 1 medium-sized head of firm cabbage

Directions:

1. Preheat the oven to 450°F and spray a baking sheet with non-stick spray or oil.
2. Remove outer leaves from the cabbage and cut it into quarters, same in size; then, cut each piece in half to get 8 wedges. Lay the cabbage wedges on the baking sheet, making sure they do not touch. Next, mix oil, Sriracha sauce, lime juice, and salt and brush the cabbage wedges with it on both sides leaving about 1/3 of the mixture.

3. Place the baking sheet into the oven and then roast for 15 to 18 minutes, until the edges begin to brown; then carefully turn the wedges and brush with the remaining mixture.
4. Roast for about 15 to 20 minutes more. Remove from the oven and trim of the core.
5. Sprinkle with sesame seeds and serve hot.

45. Dashing Shrimp and Broccoli Feast

Preparation Time: 10 minutes
Cooking Time: 20 minutes
Servings: 4
Ingredients:

- 2 tablespoons ghee
- Pepper to taste
- 7 minced garlic cloves
- Juice of 1/2 lime
- 1 lb broccoli florets
- 1/4 cup chicken broth
- 1 bay leaf
- 1.5 teaspoon fish sauce
- 2/3 cup white wine
- 2 teaspoons toasted sesame oil
- 1.5 teaspoon red pepper flakes
- 1 lb peeled and deveined shrimp

Directions:

1. First of all, melt ghee in large pan over medium heat. Add garlic and sauté until softened.
2. Add the broccoli and other vegetables wanted, sautéing for about 2 minutes. Add shrimp and bay leaf. Increase heat to medium high and add red pepper flakes, sesame oil, and fish sauce.
3. Toss everything around in the pan to coat in the mixture. Cook properly for additional 2 to 5 minutes. Pour in broth and white wine, then reduce heat back to medium.
4. Let it cook properly for about 5 to 10 more minutes until the vegetables are soft and the shrimp is opaque. Finally squeeze lime juice over it and crack fresh pepper for taste, then serve!

46. Cilantro Garlic Pork Chops

Preparation Time: 10 Minutes
Cooking Time: 15 Minutes
Servings: 4
Ingredients:

- 2 pounds pork chopped
- Salt and pepper
- ¼ cup good-quality olive oil, divided
- ¼ cup finely chopped fresh cilantro
- 1 tablespoon minced garlic
- Juice of 1 lime

Directions:

1. Marinate the pork. Pat the pork chops dry and season them lightly with salt and pepper. Place

them in a large bowl, add 2 tablespoons of the olive oil, and the cilantro, garlic, and lime juice.

2. Toss to coat the chops. Cover the bowl and marinate the chops at room temperature for 30 minutes. Cook the pork. In a large skillet over medium-high heat, warm the remaining 2 tablespoons of olive oil. Add the pork chops in a single layer and fry them, turning them once, until they're just cooked through and still juicy, 6 to 7 minutes per side.

3. Serve. Divide the chops between four plates and serve them immediately.

47. Spinach Feta Stuffed Pork

Preparation Time: 15 Minutes
Cooking Time: 30 Minutes
Servings: 4
Ingredients:
- 4 ounces crumbled feta cheese
- ¾ cup chopped frozen spinach
- 3 tablespoons chopped olives
- 4-ounce center pork chops, 2 inches thick
- Salt and pepper
- 3 tablespoons good-quality olive oil

Directions: Preheat the oven. Set the oven temperature to 400°F.

1. Make the filling. In a small bowl, mix together the feta, spinach, and olives until everything is well combined. Stuff the pork chops. Make a horizontal slit in the side of each chop to create a pocket, making sure you don't cut all the way through. Stuff the filling equally between the chops and secure the slits with toothpicks. Lightly season the stuffed chops with salt and pepper. Brown the chops. In a large oven-safe skillet over medium-high heat, warm the olive oil. Add the chops and sear them until they're browned all over, about 10 minutes in total.

2. Roast the chops. Place the skillet in the oven and roast the chops for 20 minutes or until they're cooked through. Serve. Let the meat rest for 10 minutes and then remove the toothpicks. Divide the pork chops between four plates and serve them immediately.

48. Coconut Milk Ginger Marinated Pork Tenderloin

Preparation Time: 5 Minutes   **Cooking Time:** 25 Minutes   **Servings:** 4
Ingredients:
- ¼ cup coconut oil, divided
- 1½ pounds boneless pork chopped
- 1 tablespoon grated fresh ginger
- 2 teaspoons minced garlic
- 1 cup coconut milk
- 1 teaspoon chopped basil
- Juice of 1 lime
- ½ cup shredded coconut

Directions:

1. Brown the pork. In a large skillet over medium heat, warm 2 tablespoons of the coconut oil. Add the pork chops to the skillet and brown them all over, turning them several times, about 10 minutes in total.

2. Braise the pork. Move the pork to the side of the skillet and add the remaining 2 tablespoons of coconut oil. Add the ginger and garlic and sauté until they've softened, about 2 minutes. Stir in the coconut milk, basil, and lime juice and move the pork back to the center of the skillet. Cover the skillet and simmer until the pork is just cooked through and very tender, 12 to 15 minutes. Serve the pork chops between four plates and top them with the shredded coconut.

49. Grilled Pork Chops with Greek Salsa

Preparation Time: 15 Minutes
Cooking Time: 15 Minutes
Servings: 4
Ingredients:

- ¼ cup olive oil, divided
- 1 tablespoon red wine
- 3 teaspoons chopped oregano, divided
- 1 teaspoon minced garlic
- 4-ounce boneless pork chopped
- ½ cup halved cherry tomatoes
- ½ yellow bell pepper, diced
- ½ English cucumber, chopped
- ¼ red onion, chopped
- 1 tablespoon balsamic vinegar
- Salt and pepper for seasoning

Directions:

1. Marinate the pork. In a medium bowl, stir together 3 tablespoons of the olive oil, the wine, 2 teaspoons of the oregano, and the garlic. Add the pork chops to the bowl, turning them to get them coated with the marinade. Cover the bowl and place it in the refrigerator for 30 minutes.
2. Make the salsa. While the pork is marinating, in a medium bowl, stir together the remaining 1 tablespoon of olive oil, the tomatoes, yellow bell pepper, cucumber, red onion, vinegar, and the remaining 1 teaspoon of oregano. Season the salsa with salt and pepper. Set the bowl aside.
3. Grill the pork chops. Heat a grill to medium-high heat. Remove the pork chops from the marinade and grill them until just cooked through, 6 to 8 minutes per side.
4. Serve. Rest the pork for 5 minutes. Divide the pork between four plates and serve them with a generous scoop of the salsa.

50. Grilled Herbed Pork Kebabs

Preparation Time: 10 Minutes
Cooking Time: 15 Minutes
Servings: 4
Ingredients:

- ¼ cup good-quality olive oil
- 1 tablespoon minced garlic
- 2 teaspoons dried oregano
- 1 teaspoon dried basil
- 1 teaspoon dried parsley
- Salt and pepper to taste
- 1-pound pork tenderloin, chopped

Directions:

1. Marinate the pork. In a medium bowl, stir together the olive oil, garlic, oregano, basil, parsley, salt, and pepper. Add the pork pieces and toss to coat them in the marinade. Cover the bowl and place it in the refrigerator for 2 to 4 hours.
2. Make the kebabs. Divide the pork pieces between four skewers, making sure not to crowd the meat. Grill the kebabs. Preheat your grill to medium-high heat. Grill the skewers for about 12 minutes, turning to cook all pork sides until the pork is cooked through.
3. Serve. Rest the skewers for 5 minutes. Divide the skewers between four plates and serve them immediately.

51. Pork Meat and Broccoli Sauté

Preparation Time: 10 Minutes
Cooking Time: 20 Minutes
Servings: 4
Ingredients:

- 2 tablespoons olive oil
- 2 pounds pork meat
- 4 cups small broccoli florets
- 1 tablespoon minced garlic
- Black pepper to taste

Directions:

1. Cook the sausage. In a large skillet over medium heat, warm the olive oil. Add the chop pork meat sauté it until it's cooked through, 8 to 10 minutes. Transfer the meat to a plate with a slotted spoon and set the plate aside. Sauté the vegetables. Add the broccoli to the skillet and sauté it until it's tender, about 6 minutes. Stir in the garlic and sauté for another 3 minutes.
2. Finish the dish. Return the meat to the skillet and toss to combine it with the other ingredients. Season the mixture with pepper.
3. Serve. Divide the mixture between four plates and serve it immediately.

52. Greek Beef Stew

Servings: 8
Cooking Time: 8 hours
Ingredients

- 4 pounds meat beef
- 20 whole shallots, peeled
- 3 bay leaves
- 8 garlic cloves
- 3 sprigs rosemary
- 6 whole pimento
- 5 whole cloves
- 1/2 teaspoon ground nutmeg
- 1/2 cup avocado oil
- 1/3 cup apple cider vinegar
- Salt and pepper
- 2 cups tomato paste

Instructions

Put all ingredients in the slow cooker and cook on low for 8 hours.

53. Beef, Parsnip, Celery Stew

Servings: 8
Cooking Time: 8 hours
Ingredients

- 3 pounds beef meat
- 2 chopped onions
- 6 chopped carrots
- 2 tablespoons olive oil
- 1 sprig dried thyme
- 2 chopped parsnips
- 1/2 cup brown rice
- 4 cups beef stock
- Salt and black pepper
- 1 bunch chopped parsley
- 1 bunch chives

Instructions

Put all ingredients in the slow cooker and cook on low for 8 hours.

54. Beef Meatballs with White Beans

Servings: 8
Cooking Time: 2 hours 20 minutes
Ingredients

- 2 pounds beef meat
- 2 tablespoons olive oil
- 1 sprig thyme, minced
- 2 cups uncooked white navy beans
- 4 cups beef stock
- Salt and pepper to taste
- 1 chopped onion
- 1 bunch chopped parsley
- 1 cup chopped carrots

Instructions

1. Take a pot and add 4 cups beef stock, salt, pepper, withe beans and beef meat and cook on low for 2 hours more. Turn off the heat.

2. Take a food processor and mix the beef meat mixture, thyme, chopped onion, parsley, and chopped carrots. Blend until uniform.

3. Make 16 meatballs. Add them to the bot from before and cook for 20 minutes on low. Garnish with parsley and serve!

55. Beef meat with Red Beans

Servings: 6

Cooking Time: 4 hours

Ingredients

- 3 tablespoons olive oil
- 1 chopped onion
- 1 lb cubed beef meet
- 2 teaspoons ground cumin
- 2 teaspoon turmeric
- 1 teaspoon cinnamon
- 3 cups water
- 4 tablespoons chopped fresh parsley
- 3 tablespoons snipped chives
- 2 cups cooked kidney beans
- 3 tablespoons lemon juice
- Salt and pepper to taste

Instructions

Put all ingredients in the pot and cook on low for 4 hours.

56. Lamb and Pecan Salad

Preparation Time: 10 minutes

Cooking Time: 10 minutes

Servings: 4

Ingredients:

- 2 lamb chops
- 1 tablespoon sesame oil
- 2 pecans, chopped
- 2 cups lettuce, chopped
- 1 teaspoon cayenne pepper
- 1 tablespoon avocado oil

Directions:

1. Sprinkle the lamb chops with cayenne pepper and put in the hot skillet.
2. Add sesame oil and roast the meat for 4 minutes per side. Then chops the lamb chops and put them in the salad bowl. Add all remaining ingredients and carefully mix the salad.

57. Hot Sauce Lamb

Preparation Time: 10 minutes

Cooking Time: 35 minutes

Servings: 4

Ingredients:

- 2 teaspoons paprika
- pound lamb fillet, chopped
- 1 tablespoon coconut oil
- 4 tablespoons keto hot sauce
- ½ cup of water

Directions:

1. Pour water in the saucepan and bring it to boil. Add lamb and boil it for 20 minutes.
2. After this, preheat the skillet well. Add boiled lamb fillet, coconut oil, and paprika.
3. Roast the ingredients for 6 minutes per side or until the meat is light brown. Then add hot sauce and carefully mix the meal. Serve.

Salad Recipes

58. Herbed Potato Salad

Preparation Time: 10 minutes
Cooking Time: 20 minutes
Servings: 6
Ingredients:

- Red potatoes – 1 ½ pounds
- Brown mustard – ½ tablespoon
- Fresh parsley – 1 tablespoon
- Italian dressing – ½ cup
- Black pepper – ¼ teaspoon
- Garlic salt – 1 teaspoon
- Green bell pepper – ½ cup
- Red bell pepper – ½ cup
- Green onions – ½ cup

Directions:

1. Place the potatoes in a large pot and boil for about 10 minutes. Ensure the potatoes do not become overly soft. Drain off excess water and set aside to cool.
2. Once cool, cut them into small pieces (preferably bite size) and transfer to a medium-sized bowl. Put in a small bowl the Italian dressing, parsley, black pepper and garlic salt. Add the potatoes and mix. With care, stir in green onions, green and red bell peppers. Serve.

59. Corn and Green Chili Salad

Preparation Time: 10 minutes
Cooking Time: 0 minutes
Servings: 4
Ingredients:

- Frozen corn – 2 cups
- Vegetable oil – ½ tablespoon
- Tomatoes – 1 can
- Green chilies – 1 can
- Green onions – 1/3 cup
- Lime juice – 1 tablespoon
- Fresh cilantro – 2 tablespoons

Directions:

1. Place frozen corn, diced tomatoes and chilies in a bowl. Add vegetable oil, lime juice, green onions and cilantro. Mix the ingredients thoroughly. If desired, add diced chicken when serving.

60. Black Bean and Corn Pitas

Preparation Time: 5 minutes
Cooking Time: 1 minutes.
Servings: 4
Ingredients:

- Black beans (low-sodium) – 1 can
- Tomatoes – 1 cup fresh
- Garlic (chopped) – 1
- Frozen corn – 1 cup
- Avocado (chopped) – 1
- Black pepper – 2 teaspoons
- Fresh parsley – 1 teaspoon
- Lemon juice–2 teaspoons
- Whole wheat pita– 2 mediums
- Chili powder – ½ teaspoon
- Mozzarella cheese – 1/3 cup

Directions:

1. Drain the canned black beans and rinse. Combine the beans with tomatoes, garlic, corn and avocado in a medium size bowl. Add cayenne pepper, chili powder, and parsley and lemon juice to the mix in the bowl. Cut the whole wheat pita in half to make 4 pockets.
2. Scoop the fillings into each half of the pita bread. Add cheese as toppings. Serve.

61. Chicken Tortas

Preparation Time: 15 minutes
Cooking Time: 15 minutes
Servings: 4
Ingredients:

- Chicken cooked– 2 cups
- Fresh Tomato sauce – 2 cups
- Chili powder – 1 teaspoon
- Radishes (sliced) – 2
- Romaine lettuce – 2 cups
- Low fat cheese (shredded) – ½ cup
- Avocado (mashed) – 1
- French bread rolls (cut in half) -4

Directions:

1. Combine shredded chicken, a cup of Fresh Salsa and chili powder in a medium-sized bowl. Combine shredded lettuce, cheese, radishes and onion in another medium-sized bowl. On each French bread roll spread an equal amount of avocado. Add the chicken and lettuce mix in equal amounts. Scoop a quarter Fresh Salsa over lettuce already spread on the roll. Close the roll and your sandwich is ready.

62. Avocado Garden Salad

Preparation Time: 10 minutes
Cooking Time: 20 minutes.
Servings: 6
Ingredients:

- Mixed salad vegetables – 6 cups
- Tomatoes chopped – 3
- Cucumber (peeled, chopped) – 1
- Onions (chopped) - 5
- Garlic powder – 1/3 teaspoon
- Lemon juice – 2 tablespoons
- Salt and pepper
- Avocado (peeled) – 1

Directions:

1. Place greens, cucumber, tomatoes and onions in a large bowl and mix together. Mix lemon juice, ground pepper, garlic powder and salt in a small bowl. Pour the lemon juice mix over the salad mix and toss. Prepare the avocado slices: cut into halves, remove pit, peel and slice into wedge-like shapes of about 1/8-inch thickness. Place the avocado slices over the salad. Enjoy!

63. Avocado and Chicken Egg Salad Sandwich

Preparation Time: 10 minutes
Cooking Time: 0 minutes.
Servings: 6
Ingredients:

- 2 eggs – hard-boiled, chopped
- 2 egg whites – hard-boiled, chopped
- 1 shredded chicken breast – cooked
- 2 avocados – small, peeled
- Greek yogurt – 1 tablespoon
- Green onion – 2 tablespoons
- Lemon juice – 1 tablespoon
- Dijon mustard – ¼ tablespoon
- Salt and pepper

Directions:

1. Put the eggs, chicken, avocados, egg whites, Greek yogurt, green onion, lemon juice and mustard in a bowl. Mash the combination with a fork and add salt and pepper to taste. Enjoy!

64. Tuna Apple Salad

Preparation Time: 15 minutes
Cooking Time: 0 minutes
Servings: 6

Ingredients:

- Water-packed tuna – 6 ounces

- 1 Medium apple (chopped)
- Red onion (chopped) – 2 tablespoons
- Celery (chopped) – ¼ cup
- Golden raisins – ¼ cup
- Salad greens – 2 cups
- Italian dressing – 3 tablespoons
- Whole wheat pita – 2

Directions:
1. Place tuna, apple, onion and raisins in a small bowl. Add 2 tablespoons of dressing and stir. Toss salad greens with 1 tablespoon of dressing in a medium-sized bowl. Cut pitas into two and fill each with equal amounts of tuna salad and salad greens. Enjoy!

65. Chicken Tomatillo Salad

Preparation Time: 10 minutes
Cooking Time: 20minutes
Servings: 5
Ingredients:
FOR SALAD:
- Cooked chicken (chopped) – 2 cups
- Frozen corn (thawed) – 1 cup
- Red bell pepper (chopped) – 1 cup
- Carrots (chopped) – 1 cup
- Green onions (sliced) – 4
- Fresh cilantro (chopped) – ¼ cup

FOR DRESSING:
- Tomatillos (husked, quartered) – 1 cup
- Anaheim chili (seeded, chopped) – 1
- Italian dressing – 3 tablespoons
- Black pepper (ground) – ½ teaspoon

Directions:
1. Put tomatillos, Italian dressing, ground pepper and Anaheim salad in a blender and mash. Combine chopped chicken, thawed frozen corn, chopped carrots, sliced green onions, chopped bell pepper and chopped cilantro in a bowl and toss. Place the dressing over the salad and toss very well. Toss until it coats, then cover and store in a fridge. You can serve it the next day with lettuce on its side.

66. Zesty Asian Chicken Salad

Preparation Time: 5 minutes
Cooking Time: 20 minutes
Servings: 4
Ingredients:
- 3 Chicken breasts boneless and cooked
- Small broccoli florets – ½ cups
- Carrots (peeled, cut in strips) – 2
- Green onions (sliced) – 3
- Red bell pepper (cut in strips) – 1
- Cabbage (shredded) – 2 cups
- Orange juice (100%) – ¼ cup
- Sesame salad dressing
- Fresh cilantro (chopped) – ¼ cup

Directions:
1. Prepare the chicken: cut into tiny strips, and place in a medium-sized bowl. Cook it. Place broccoli florets, red bell pepper, carrots, and cabbage and green onions in the bowl. Mix orange juice and dressing together in a small bowl. Pour the dressing mixture over the salad. Toss until it coats. Add cilantro and stir. Enjoy!

67. Yummy Cucumber and Tomato Salad

Preparation Time: 20 minutes
Cooking Time: 0 minutes
Servings: 5
Ingredients:
- 1 tsp black pepper
- 1 cup olives

- 1.5 tbsp. fresh Basil, sliced
- 2 tbsps. Olive Oil
- 1 tbsp. oregano, minced
- 2.5 tbsps. Balsamic Vinegar
- 2 cups Cucumber, chopped
- 2 cups Grape Tomatoes
- 1 clove Garlic, minced

Directions:

1. First of all, rinse and peel cucumber. Use julienne peeler to make noodles from the flesh of the cucumber. Stop when you get down to the seeds; then rinse grape tomatoes, slice in half. Thinly slice basil, chop oregano, and mince garlic. Finally toss all ingredients with the Kalamata olives in a medium mixing bowl, drizzle with olive oil and balsamic vinegar, and sprinkle with pepper.

68. Astonishing Strawberry Mint Salad

Preparation Time: 2 to 5 minutes

Cooking Time: 5 to 10 minutes

Servings: 1 to 2

Ingredients:

- Fresh lemon juice – about 1.5 tablespoon
- Skinned and chopped cucumber – 2 cups
- Pinch of salt
- Fresh mint – 1/2 cup
- Olive oil – 2 tablespoons
- Chopped strawberries – 2 cups

Directions:

1. First of all, skin and chop the cucumbers
2. Chop the strawberries and the fresh mint.
3. Finally add all to a bowl then serve.

Festival and Special Occasion Meals

69. Chicken and Sweet Potato Bake

Preparation Time: 15 minutes
Cooking Time: 35 minutes.
Servings: 3 – 4
Ingredients:

- Chicken breasts boneless – 1 lb.
- Broccoli floret – 4 cups
- 1 large sweet potato – cubed
- Red onion – 3 cups, chopped
- Garlic – 2 cloves, minced
- Olive oil – 1/3 cup
- Dried cranberries – ¼ cup
- Salt and pepper to taste
- Italian seasoning – 1 teaspoon

Directions:

1. Preheat your oven to 400°F, and line a baking sheet with a parchment paper. Combine the sweet potato, garlic, broccoli, onion and cranberries on a pain. Sprinkle olive oil over them and add salt and pepper. Toss the ingredients on the pan, and cover with a foil. Put in the oven and allow to it bake for about 12 minutes. Remove from the oven after twelve minutes and add the chicken. Toss and place in the oven. Allow it to bake for about 20 minutes or alternatively, until the chicken is completely cooked, and the potatoes are completely soft. Serve.

70. Apple Turkey Gyro

Preparation Time: 10 minutes
Cooking Time: 25 minutes
Servings: 6
Ingredients:

- Turkey breast – ½ pound
- Apple (cored, sliced) – 1
- Onion (sliced) –1 cup
- Green bell pepper sliced – 2
- Red bell pepper sliced – 2
- Lemon juice – 1 tablespoon
- Vegetable oil – 1 tablespoon
- Whole wheat pita toasted – 6
- Low fat plain yogurt– ½ cup

Directions:

1. Cut the turkey into thin slices. Spray a skillet or a pan with non-stick spraying oil. Stir fry onion, green and red bell peppers and lemon juice in it until they appear crisp and tender.
2. Add the turkey and allow it to cook through. Turn off the heat or remove the pan or skillet from heat. Add apple and stir. Fill a folded pita with the mix. Serve. Drizzle with plain yogurt.

71. Vegetable Quesadillas

Preparation Time: 10 minutes
Cooking Time: 25 minutes
Servings: 4
Ingredients:

- Frozen corn – 1 or 2 cups
- Flour tortillas – 4
- Green onion, sliced – ½
- Green bell pepper chopped – ½
- Tomato chopped – ½
- Cilantro chopped – 2 tablespoons
- Reduced-fat Cheddar – ½ cup
- Non-stick cooking spray

Directions:

1. Spray a medium-sized skillet with the cooking spray and stir fry corn and green pepper in heat over low heat for about 5 minutes. Add chopped tomato and sliced green onion and continue

to cook. Add chopped cilantro when the vegetables have been heated through. Stir frequently.

2. Place tortillas in a large skillet and heat on high. Place the cooked vegetables and cheese in equal amount on each tortilla and fold over. Cook until the cheese melts and the tortillas appear slightly brown and crisp. Serve.

72. Delicious Chicken Curry

Servings: 6
Cooking Time: 1 hour
Ingredients

- 2 pounds chicken meat, chopped
- 2 tablespoons curry
- 2 cups tomato paste
- 1/2 cup heavy cream
- Salt to taste
- 1/2 cup of water
- Cilantro for garnishing

Instructions

1.In a bowl, mix chicken chopped in the curry powder. Add the tomato paste, salt and the cream. Stir to combine. Take a pot add 1/2 cups of water. Stir in and cook on low for 1 hour. Stir often and add water if needed. Serve with cilantro for garnish.

73. Chickpea Curry

Servings: 4
Ingredients

- 3 tablespoons curry
- 4 cups cooked chickpeas
- 1 cup chopped cilantro

Instructions

1.Put all ingredients in the slow cooker and cook on low for 4 hours.

74. Ratatouille

Servings: 6
Ingredients

- 2 large eggplants, sliced
- 2 medium onions, sliced
- 1 red pepper, sliced
- 1 green pepper, sliced
- 4 large tomatoes, sliced
- 2 garlic cloves, sliced
- 4 tablespoons olive oil
- 1 tablespoon fresh basil
- Salt and pepper to taste

Instructions

1.Put all ingredients in the slow cooker and cook on low for 4 hours

75. Eggplant, Zucchini and Tomato

Servings: 4
Cooking Time: 4 hours
Ingredients

- 2 cups sliced zucchini
- 2 cups sliced tomatoes
- 2 tablespoons olive oil
- 2 cups sliced eggplant
- salt and pepper to taste
- ½ tsp. minced garlic

Instructions

1.Arrange all ingredients in the slow cooker dish, cover and cook on low for 4 hours.

76. Menacing Goulash

Preparation Time: 10 minutes   **Cooking Time:** 15 minutes   **Servings:** 4

Ingredients:

- 2 pounds of lean ground beef
- 13 teaspoons of olive oil
- 1 red bell pepper, seeded, chopped
- 1 onion cut up into short strips
- 1 tablespoon of minced garlic
- 2 tablespoons of sweet paprika
- ½ a teaspoon of hot paprika
- 4 cups of beef stock
- 2 cans of petite diced tomatoes

Directions:

1. Take your pot and add 2 teaspoon of olive oil on the bottom. Add the ground beef. Cook it to break it up; once the beef is browned, transfer it to a bowl.
2. Apart from, cut the stem off your pepper, remove the seed and cut it into short strips; cut your onion into short strips. Add extra teaspoon of olive oil, the onions and pepper to your pot.
3. Sauté them for about 3-4 minutes. Add the minced garlic, hot paprika, sweet paprika and cook it for 2-3 minutes. Add the beef stock along with the petite tomatoes. Add the ground beef and close the lid. Allow it to cook for about 15 minutes on low fire. Once it is done, enjoy!

77. Luxurious Rotisserie Chicken

Preparation Time: 5 minutes
Cooking Time: 25 minutes
Servings: 6
Ingredients:

- 1 whole chicken
- 1 ½ teaspoon of salt
- 1 teaspoon of minced garlic
- ½ a teaspoon of pepper
- 1 ½ tablespoon avocado oil
- 1 yellow quartered onion
- 1 halved lemon
- 1 cup of chicken broth

Directions:

1. Remove the parts from your chicken cavity and rinse it well. Pat it dries with a paper towel.
2. Take a pot and add the spices, salt and pepper to it. Stir properly. Add the oil to your spices and stir properly until it mixes fully. Rub the breast with oil and spice the mix. Add the chicken breast and heat it for 5-7 minutes until it gets fully crispy. Flip the breast and crisp the other side for about a minute. Add chicken stock. Cover and cook for 25 minutes. Stir frequently.
3. Turn off the heat, but don't remove the lid for 5-6 minutes. Then, transfer the chicken to your serving plate. Let it rest for 5 minutes and serve by pouring a bit of the cooking liquid on top.

78. Whispering Meal of Lamb

Preparation Time: 10 minutes
Cooking Time: 30 minutes
Servings: 4
Ingredients:

- 2 tablespoons of ghee
- 1 diced onion
- 4 minced garlic cloves
- ½ fresh ginger minced
- 1-2 Serrano peppers minced
- 4 chopped tomatoes
- 1 tablespoon of coriander
- 1 teaspoon of paprika
- Salt and pepper to taste
- ½ a teaspoon of cumin powder
- ½ a teaspoon of chili powder
- ¼ teaspoon of turmeric powder
- 1 pound of ground lamb
- 1 cup of rinsed frozen peas
- 3 chopped carrots
- 2 chopped potatoes
- 1 can of tomato sauce
- Cilantro for garnish

Directions:

1. Take your pot and add the ghee to melt on low. Add the onion and saute them until they get brown thoroughly; then add the garlic, ginger, Serrano pepper and stir properly.
2. Put the tomatoes and cook it for an additional minute. Add the spices and fry it for 1 minute.
3. Place the ground lamb into the pot and cook until it gets fully browned.
4. Add the peas, carrots, tomato sauce, potatoes and mix everything properly. Cover and cook it for about 30 minutes. Stir frequently. If it needs add a bit of water. Turn off the heat but don't remove the lid for 3-4 minutes to allow the heat to release naturally. Serve and enjoy!

79. Succulent Maple Smoked Brisket

Preparation Time: 10 minutes
Cooking Time: 50 minutes
Servings: 5
Ingredients:

- 1 ½ pound of beef brisket
- 2 tablespoons of maple sugar
- Salt and pepper
- 1 teaspoon of mustard powder
- 1 teaspoon of onion powder
- ½ a teaspoon of smoked paprika
- 2 cups of bone broth
- 1 tablespoon of liquid smoke
- 3 fresh thyme sprigs

Directions:

1. Remove the brisket from your fridge for 30 minutes before cooking and pat it dry using paper towels. Take a bowl, add the maple sugar, sea salt, mustard powder, pepper, onion powder, smoked paprika and mix them properly to prepare the spice blender.
2. Take your pot and grease up the bottom using oil. Add the brisket and cook it until it gets brown. Turn the brisket to the fatty side; add the liquid smoke, broth and thyme.
3. Scrape off the browned bits. Cover and cook for about 50 minutes. Stir frequently.
4. Once it is done, turn off the heat, but don't remove the lid to allow the heat to release naturally for 5 minutes. Saute and wait for 10 minutes for the sauce to get thickened. Remove the brisket from the pot and allow it rest. Slice up the brisket; serve it with sauce and whipped veggies.

80. Yummy Cucumber and Tomato Salad

Preparation Time: 20 minutes
Cooking Time: 0 minutes
Servings: 5
Ingredients:

- 1 tsp black pepper
- 1 cup olives
- 1.5 tbsp. fresh Basil, sliced
- 2 tbsps. Olive Oil
- 1 tbsp. oregano, minced
- 2.5 tbsps. Balsamic Vinegar
- 2 cups Cucumber, chopped
- 2 cups Grape Tomatoes
- 1 clove Garlic, minced

Directions:

First of all, rinse and peel cucumber. Use julienne peeler to make noodles from the flesh of the cucumber. Stop when you get down to the seeds; then rinse grape tomatoes, slice in half. Thinly slice basil, chop oregano, and mince garlic. Finally toss all ingredients with the Kalamata olives in a medium mixing bowl, drizzle with olive oil and balsamic vinegar, and sprinkle with pepper.

81. Living Breathing Rice Pudding

Preparation Time: 5 minutes

Cooking Time: 10 minutes

Servings: 8

Ingredients:

- 1 cup of Arborio rice
- 1 and a ½ cup of water
- ¼ teaspoon of salt
- 2 cups of divided whole milk
- ½ a cup of sugar
- 2 pieces of eggs
- ½ teaspoon of vanilla extract
- ¾ cup of raisins

Directions:

1. Add the rice, the water and salt to your pot. Cover and cook it for about 3 minutes on high heat. After this, turn down the heat and add 1 and a ½ cup of milk with the sugar to your rice. Stir properly. Take a small sized mixing bowl; whisk in the eggs and ½ a cup of milk alongside vanilla. Pour the mixture through a metal mesh into your pot. Simmer until it starts to boil.
2. Turn the heat off and remove the pot. Add the raisins. Let it cool off, as it will thicken the pudding. Serve it warm with toppings of whipped cream, nutmeg or cinnamon. Enjoy!

82. Kid's Favorite Chocolate Fondue

Preparation Time: 2 minutes

Cooking Time: 10 minutes

Servings: 4

Ingredients:

- 3.5 ounces of Swiss Chocolate
- 3 and a ½ ounce of Fresh Cream
- 1 teaspoon of sugar
- 1 teaspoon of Amaretto liquor
- 2 cups of water

Directions:

1. Add 2 cups of water to your pot. Take a small sized heat proof ramekin and add the chocolate chunks. Add the same amount of fresh cream, liquor and sugar. Lower it into your pot.
2. Close the lid and cook it for about 2 minutes on medium heat. Turn off the heat, but don't remove the lid for 5-6 minutes to allow the heat to release naturally. Take it out using tongs or gloves. Stir the contents vigorously for 1 minute. Serve immediately!

83. Ultimate Pan-Fried Lemon Chicken

Preparation Time: 15 minutes

Cooking Time: 15 minutes

Servings: 5

Ingredients:

- Zest and juice of 1 lemon
- Fat of choice
- 1.5 teaspoons olive oil
- Salt and pepper
- 1 chicken breast

Directions:

1. Zest the lemon and squeeze the juice. Add chicken breast, olive oil, lemon zest and juice, salt and pepper to a cooking-zip lock bag. Seal the bag, squeezing out the air.
2. Next, please flatten the chicken with a meat pounder or maybe rolling pin, so it is even in thickness. Set it aside for about 30 to 35 minutes or cook immediately; then add oil or other fat of choice to a skillet and heat over medium-high heat. Remove the chicken from the bag and add to the skillet. Fry the chicken on both sides for about 2 to 5 minutes on each or until cooked. Wait about 5 to 10 minutes before slicing. Serve!

84. Skillet Moroccan Chicken

Preparation Time: 10 minutes

Cooking Time: 20 minutes

Servings: 2

Ingredients:

- 2 chicken breasts
- ½ tbsp. extra-virgin olive oil
- 2 cups cauliflower, chopped
- ½ cup sweet onion, chopped
- 1 carrot peeled and sliced
- 2 Medjool dates, sliced
- ½ cup cilantro, chopped
- ½ small cucumber, thinly sliced
- ¾ cup fresh orange juice
- ½ cup crushed tomatoes
- 15 roasted pistachios, chopped
- 1½ tsp. fresh ginger, minced
- 1 tsp. ground cinnamon
- 1½ tsp. ground cumin
- ¼ tsp. paprika
- 1/8 tsp. ground allspice
- Salt and pepper, to taste

TO GARNISH:

- Cilantro, chopped

Directions:

1. Using a meat mallet pound the chicken breasts until they are quite flat and season with salt and pepper. Heat the olive oil in a large skillet on a medium-high heat. Cook the chicken until golden brown, about 1-1.5 minutes. Turnover and repeat on the other side and transfer to a plate, tenting with aluminum foil to keep warm. Lower the heat to medium and add the onion, ginger, carrot, cauliflower, cumin, paprika, cinnamon, and allspice to the pan. Cook for 3 minutes. stirring continuously until the veggies just begin to soften and the spices turn fragrant.

2. Stir in the crushed tomatoes, orange juice, and sliced Medjool dates. Turn the heat up to high and bring the stew and boil for 2 minutes; then lower the heat to medium and simmer for 5 minutes, stirring, until the sauce begins to reduce and thicken. Season to taste.

3. Return the chicken back into the skillet and spoon the sauce over top. Cover and reduce the heat to medium-low and cook until the chicken is no longer pink, for about 10 minutes. Stir in the fresh cilantro and serve the chicken in two plates. Top each serving with chopped pistachios and place the sliced cucumbers on the side. Garnish with extra cilantro and enjoy!

85. One-Pot Steak Potato and Pepper

Preparation Time: 5 minutes

Cooking Time: 50 minutes

Servings: 2-3

Ingredients:

- 1 tbsp. butter
- 1 lb. sirloin steak, chopped
- 1 large Korean yam, chopped

TO GARNISH:

- Chopped fresh cilantro
- 8 yellow/red/green sweet peppers, sliced
- 2 tbsps. extra-virgin olive oil
- 1 small red onion, thinly sliced
- 1 tsp. smoked paprika
- ½ tsp. garlic powder
- Salt and pepper to taste

Directions:

1. Place the butter on the bottom of a large pot and heat on medium until the butter has melted. Swirl the pan so that the butter coats the entire surface. Place all the ingredients into the pot,

toss well to combine and cook on medium for 50 minutes. Stir and check frequently to ensure even cooking. Once it is ready, sprinkle with chopped fresh cilantro and serve.

86. Protein-Rich English Breakfast

Preparation Time: 5 minutes
Cooking Time: 30 minutes
Servings: 2
Ingredients:

- 2 eggs
- 4 thinly slices pork meat
- 2 purple sweet potatoes
- 1 tomato
- ½ lb. mushrooms

TO GARNISH:

- Red chili flakes
- Fresh herbs
- Salt and pepper, to taste

Directions:

1. Preheat the oven to 400° Fahrenheit. Take a baking dish with parchment paper. Place the chopped sweet purple potatoes and bake for 15 minutes.
2. In a cast iron skillet, cook on medium the pork meat for 10 minutes. Remove from the skillet, set aside and drain off any extra fat. Slice the tomato and roughly chop the mushrooms. Cook the mushrooms in the same skillet that cooked the meat. When the mushrooms have cooked down, add the tomato slices and cook quickly on high. Remove the mushrooms and tomato slices from the skillet and set onto a plate. Fry the eggs; add a little more oil to ensure they don't stick. Slice open the sweet potatoes and place them on a plate with the cooked meat, tomato slices, mushrooms, and eggs. Garnish with salt, pepper, herbs, and red chili flakes. Enjoy hot.

87. Delicious Apple Crisp

Preparation Time: 15 minutes
Cooking Time: 30 minutes
Servings: 8
Ingredients:
FOR THE APPLES:

- 6 apples, peeled and sliced thinly
- 2 tbsps. coconut oil
- ¼ cup maple syrup
- ¼ cup water, if needed
- 1 tsp. ground cinnamon
- ½ tsp. ground nutmeg

FOR THE CRUMBLE TOPPING:

- ¼ cup solid coconut oil
- ½ cup unsweetened coconut
- ½ cup walnuts
- ½ cup sliced almonds
- ¼ cup coconut sugar

Directions:

1. Preheat the oven to 350° F.
2. In a cast iron skillet, melt the coconut oil or butter over medium-high heat. Add apples and cook for about 5 minutes, stirring occasionally. Mix in the maple syrup, nutmeg and cinnamon and add a quarter cup of water if mixture turns out dry. Continue to cook for 3-5 minutes, until apples are tender, but not too mushy; then remove from heat and set aside.
3. Meanwhile the in a medium bowl, combine the almonds, walnuts, coconut, and coconut sugar. Stir in the coconut oil until well combined. Sprinkle the crumble over the cooked apples in the skillet. Bake at 350° F for 15-20 minutes or until the topping turns a light golden brown.
4. Serve warm, topped with dairy-free ice cream if desired.

88. Pepper Steak

Servings: 6
Cooking Time: 6 hours
Ingredients

- 2 pounds beef sirloin, chopped
- 1 garlic clove, minced
- 3 tablespoons olive oil
- 2 cups Beef Broth
- ¼ cup tapioca flour
- ½ cup chopped onion
- 2 cups carrots
- 1 cup chopped tomatoes
- Salt

Instructions

1.Sprinkle beef with minced garlic. Heat the oil in a skillet and brown the seasoned beef sirloin strips. Transfer to a pot. Add carrots, onion, chopped tomatoes and salt. Mix in tapioca flour in broth until dissolved. Pour broth into the slow cooker with meat. Cover and cook on medium for 6.

89. Beef Bourguignonne

Servings 8
Cooking Time: 6 hours
Ingredients

- 4 pounds cubed lean beef
- 1 cup red wine
- 13 tablespoons olive oil
- 1 spring thyme, minced
- Salt and pepper to taste
- 2 garlic cloves, minced
- 1 onion, diced
- 1-pound mushrooms, sliced
- 1/2 cup tapioca flour

Instructions

1.Marinate beef in wine, oil, thyme and pepper for 3 hours at room temperature. Add beef with marinade and all other ingredients to a pot. Cook on low for 6 hours.

90. Tasty Chicken

Servings 6
Cooking time: 6 hours
Ingredients

- 1 whole skinless chicken
- 1/4 cup almond flour
- Salt and pepper to taste
- 1/2 cup chicken broth
- 1/2 cup sliced mushrooms
- 1 teaspoon paprika
- 2 zucchinis, chopped
- Parsley to garnish

Instructions

1.Season chicken with 1 tsp. salt. Combine flour, pepper, remaining salt, and paprika. Coat chicken pieces with this mixture. Place zucchini first in a crockpot. Pour broth over zucchini. Arrange chicken on top. Cover and cook on low for 6 hours. Turn control to high, add mushrooms, cover, and cook on high for additional 10-15 minutes. Garnish with parsley and pepper.

91. Beef Ratatouille

Servings: 8
Ingredients

- 2 cups sliced zucchini
- 1 chopped onion
- 2 sliced eggplants
- 1 sliced red pepper
- 2 tablespoons olive oil

- 2 garlic cloves, chopped
- Salt and pepper to taste
- 4 pounds cubed beef

Instructions

1. Put ingredients in the pot. Cover, and cook on low for 6 hours.

92. Lemon Roast Chicken

Servings: 6

Cooking Time: 6 hours

Ingredients

- 1 whole skinless chicken
- Salt and pepper to taste
- 2 teaspoons Oregano
- 2 garlic cloves minced
- 2 tablespoons olive oil
- 1/2 cup Water
- 3 tablespoons lemon juice
- 1 spring Rosemary, minced

Instructions

1. Add all ingredients to a pot. Cover and cook on low for 6 hours.
2. Add lemon juice when cooking is done and serve!

93. Spinach with Bacon and Shallots

Preparation Time: 10 minutes

Cooking Time: 30 minutes

Servings: 4

Ingredients:

- 16 oozes raw spinach
- ½ cup chopped white onion
- ½ cup chopped shallot
- ½ pound raw bacon slices
- 2 tbsps. butter

Directions:

1. Slice the bacon strips into small narrow pieces. In a skillet, heat the butter and add the chopped onion, shallots and bacon. Sauté for 15-20 minutes or until the onions start to caramelize and the bacon is cooked. Add the spinach and sauté on a medium heat. Stir frequently to ensure the leaves touch the skillet while cooking. Cover and steam for around 5 minutes, stir and continue until wilted. Serve!

94. Bread-Wrapped Chicken Skewers

Preparation Time: 5 minutes   **Cooking Time:** 8 minutes   **Servings:** 2

Ingredients:

- 5 chicken breasts
- 10 slices bread
- A glass of Seed Oil

Directions:

1. Take a pan and add oil on the bottom. Heat on high the oil for 2-3 minutes.
2. Cut the chopped chicken breasts into four pieces. Slice the bread in half. Wrap the bread over the meat and mix. Fry them for 4-5 minutes until browned. Serve immediately.

95. Roasted Brussels Sprouts and Bacon

Preparation Time: 20 minutes

Cooking Time: 45 minutes

Servings: 2

Ingredients:

- 24 oozes brussels sprouts
- ¼ cup fish sauce
- ¼ cup bacon grease
- 6 strips bacon

- Pepper to taste

Directions:

1. De-stem and quarter the brussels sprouts. Mix them with the bacon grease and fish sauce.
2. Slice the bacon into small strips and cook. Add the bacon and pepper to the sprouts. Spread onto a greased skillet and cook on high for 25 minutes. Stir every 5 minutes or so. Broil for a few more minutes and serve.

96. Hillbilly Cheese Surprise

Preparation Time: 15 minutes
Cooking Time: 40 minutes
Servings: 6
Ingredients:

- 4 cups broccoli florets
- ¼ cup ranch dressing
- ½ cup sharp cheese, shredded
- ¼ cup heavy whipping cream
- Salt and pepper to taste

Directions:

1. Preheat your oven to 375°F/190°C. In a bowl, combine all of the ingredients until the broccoli is well-covered. In a casserole dish, spread out the broccoli mixture.
2. Bake for 30 minutes. Take out of your oven and mix. If the florets are not tender, bake for another 5 minutes until tender. Serve!

97. Parmesan and Garlic Cauliflower

Preparation Time: 20 minutes
Cooking Time: 40 minutes
Servings: 4
Ingredients:

- 3/4 cup cauliflower florets
- 2 tbsps. butter
- 1 clove garlic, sliced thinly
- 2 tbsps. shredded parmesan
- 1 pinch of salt

Directions:

1. Preheat your oven to 350°F/175°C. On a low heat, melt the butter with the garlic in a small pot for 5-10 minutes. Strain the garlic in a sieve. Add it, the cauliflower, parmesan and salt in a baking dish. Bake for 20 minutes or until golden. Serve warm.

98. Jalapeño Guacamole

Preparation Time: 10 minutes   **Cooking Time:** 30 minutes   **Servings:** 4
Ingredients:

- 2 Hass avocados, ripe
- ¼ red onion
- 1 jalapeño
- 1 tbsp lime juice
- Sea salt

Directions:

1. Spoon the avocado innings into a bowl. Dice the jalapeño and onion. Mash the avocado to the desired consistency. Add in the onion, jalapeño and lime juice. Sprinkle with salt. Serve.

99. Green Beans and Almonds

Preparation Time: 10 minutes
Cooking Time: 15 minutes
Servings: 4
Ingredients:

- 1 lb green beans, trimmed
- 2 tbsps. butter
- ¼ cup sliced almonds
- 2 tsps. lemon pepper

Directions:

2. Steam the green beans for 8 minutes, until tender, then drain. On a medium heat, melt the butter in a skillet. Sauté the almonds until browned. Sprinkle with salt and pepper. Mix in the green beans. Serve.

100. Grain-free Tortilla Chips

Preparation Time: 15 Minutes
Cooking Time: 16 Minutes
Servings: 6
Ingredients:

- 1½ cup mozzarella cheese
- ½ cup of almond flour
- 1 tbsp. golden flaxseed meal
- Salt and pepper, to taste

Directions:

1. Preheat the oven to 375° F. Line 2 large baking sheets with parchment paper.
2. In a microwave-safe bowl, add the cheese and microwave for about 1 minute, stirring after every 15 seconds. In the bowl of melted cheese, add the almond flour, flaxseed meal, salt, and black pepper and with a fork, mix well. With your hands, knead until a dough form. Make 2 equal sized balls from the dough. Place 1 dough ball onto each prepared baking sheet and roll into an 8x10-inch rectangle. Cut each dough rectangle into triangle-shaped chips. Arrange the chips in a single layer. Bake for about 10-15 minutes, flipping once halfway through.
3. Remove from oven and set aside to cool before serving.

101. Sheet Pan Jalapeño Burgers

Preparation Time: 10 Minutes
Cooking Time: 20 Minutes
Servings: 4
Ingredients:

- 24 oozes ground beef
- Sea salt and pepper, to taste
- ½ tsp. garlic powder
- 6 slices bacon, halved
- 1 med. onion, sliced
- 2 jalapeños, seeded and sliced
- 4 slices pepper jack cheese
- ¼ cup of mayonnaise
- 1 tbsp. chili sauce
- ½ tsp. Worcestershire sauce
- 8 lbs. leaves of butter lettuce
- 8 dill pickle chips

Directions:

1. Preheat the oven to 425° F and line a baking sheet with non-stick foil. Mix the salt, pepper, and garlic into the ground beef and form 4 patties out of it. Line the burgers, bacon slices, jalapeño slices, and onion rounds onto the baking sheet and bake for about 18 minutes.
2. Top each patty with a piece of cheese and set the oven to boil. Broil for 2 minutes, then remove the pan from the oven. Serve one patty with 3 pieces of bacon, jalapeño slices, onion rounds, and desired amount of sauce with 2 pickle chips and 2 parts of lettuce. Enjoy!

Delicious Soups, Stews, Chilies

102. Chicken Turnip Soup

Preparation Time: 10 minutes
Cooking Time: 6 to 8 hours
Servings: 5
Ingredients:
- 340g bone-in chicken
- ¼ cup turnip, chopped
- ¼ cup onions, chopped
- 4 garlic cloves, smashed
- 4 cups water
- 3 sprigs thyme
- 2 bay leaves
- Salt, and pepper to taste

Directions:

1. Put the chicken, turnip, onions, garlic, water, thyme springs, and bay leaves in a pot. Season with salt and pepper, then give the mixture a good stir. Cover and cook on low for 6 to 8 hours until the chicken is cooked through. Stir frequently. When ready, remove the bay leaves and shred the chicken with a fork. Divide the soup among five bowls and serve.

103. Brown Rice Mushrooms Vegetarian Stew

Servings: 6
Cooking Time: 4 hours
Ingredients
- 2 chopped onions
- 2 tablespoons olive oil
- 1 sprig thyme, minced
- 4 chopped carrots
- 1 cup brown rice
- 2 cups mushrooms, sliced
- 4 cups chicken stock
- Salt and pepper to taste
- 1 bunch chopped parsley

Instructions

1.Put all ingredients in the slow cooker and cook on low for 4 hours.

104. Black Bean, Chicken & Brown Rice Stew

Servings: 8
Cooking Time: 4 hours
Ingredients
- 1 cup brown rice
- 1 chopped onion
- 2 tablespoons olive oil
- 1 cup uncooked black beans
- Salt, and pepper
- 1 teaspoon ground cumin
- 4 cups chicken stock
- 4 pounds chicken breast, chopped

Instructions

1.Put ingredients in the pot. Cover, and cook on low for 4 hours.

105. Pork White Bean Chili

Servings: 8
Cooking Time: 4 hours
Ingredients
- 2 red peppers, sliced
- 2 chopped onions
- 2 tablespoons olive oil
- 1 cup uncooked white beans
- 1/2 sliced jalapeno peppers
- 1 cup sweet corn
- Salt and pepper
- 2 teaspoons ground cumin
- 3 cups beef stock
- 4 pounds chopped pork meat

Instructions

1.Put ingredients in the pot. Cover, and cook on low for 4 hours.

106. Pork Meat Stew

Servings: 8
Cooking Time: 3 hours 30 minutes
Ingredients

- 3 large tomatoes, sliced
- 1 chopped onion
- 2 tablespoons olive oil
- 2 large red peppers, sliced
- 1 bunch chopped parsley
- Salt and pepper
- 2 teaspoons ground cumin
- 1 cup beef stock
- 4 pounds cubed pork meat

Instructions

Put ingredients in the pot. Cover, and cook on low for 3 hours 30 minutes.

107. Lamb & Zucchini Stew

Servings: 8
Cooking Time: 3 hours
Ingredients

- 2 medium zucchinis, sliced
- 1 cup chopped onions
- 2 tablespoons olive oil
- 2 sliced tomatoes
- 2 yellow peppers, sliced
- 2 sprigs rosemary, minced
- Salt and pepper
- 1 teaspoon cumin
- 1 cup beef stock
- 4 pounds cubed lamb meat

Instructions

Put ingredients in the one pot. Cover, and cook on low for 3 hours.

108. Chicken, Garlic & Tomato Stew

Servings: 8
Cooking Time: 2 hours 30 minutes.
Ingredients

- 3 tomatoes, chopped
- 2 chopped onions
- 2 tablespoons olive oil
- 1 garlic bulb, cutted
- Salt and pepper
- 2 teaspoons cumin
- 1 garlic clove
- 4 pounds chicken breast, chopped

Instructions

1.Put ingredients in the pot. Cover, and cook on low for 2 hours 30 minutes.

109. Chicken & Onion Stew

Servings: 8
Cooking Time: 4 hours
Ingredients

- 1 cup sliced mushrooms
- 6 large onions, chopped
- 2 tablespoons olive oil
- Salt and pepper to taste
- 2 cups chicken stock
- 4 pounds chicken breast

Instructions

1.Put ingredients in the pot. Cover, and cook on low for 4 hours.

110. Pork Stew with Plums

Servings: 6
Cooking Time: 6 hours
Ingredients

- 1 cup chopped onions
- 2 tablespoons olive oil
- 3 pounds chopped pork meat

- 2 chopped carrots
- 1 1/2 cup chicken stock
- 1/2 cup red wine
- Salt and pepper to taste
- 2 cups halved ripe plums, stoned
- 2 garlic cloves

Instructions

1.Add all ingredients to pot and cover with the lid. Cook on low for 6 hours.

111. Chicken Mushrooms & Olives Stew

Servings: 6

Cooking Time: 6 hours

Ingredients

- 4 pounds chicken with skin on
- 3 large chopped carrots
- 1 chopped onion
- 2 tablespoons olive oil
- 1 cup sliced mushrooms
- 1/2 cup chopped celery
- 1 cup black olives
- Salt and pepper to taste
- 1 garlic clove, minced
- ½ cup fresh parsley

Instructions

1.Put all ingredients in the crockpot, cover and cook on low 6 hours.

112. Pork, Celery and Basil Stew

Servings: 8

Cooking Time: 8 hours

Ingredients

- 1 chopped onion
- 2 Tablespoons coconut oil
- 3 pounds chopped pork meat
- 3 chopped carrots
- 2 1/2 cups beef stock
- 1 cup red wine
- Salt and pepper to taste
- 1 bunch chopped parsley
- 1 cup chopped celery
- 1/2 cup fresh basil

Instructions

1.Add all ingredients to slow cooker and cook on low for 8 hours.

113. Irish Stew

Servings: 8

Cooking Time: 5 hours

Ingredients

- 2 chopped onions
- 3 tablespoons olive oil
- 1 sprig thyme
- 3 pounds chopped lamb meat
- 4 chopped carrots
- 1/2 cup brown rice
- 6 cups chicken stock
- Salt and pepper to taste
- 1 tablespoon minced parsley
- 1 tablespoon minced bay leaf
- 3 chopped sweet potatoes
- 1 bunch chopped parsley
- 1 bunch chives

Instructions

1.Put all ingredients in the slow cooker and cook on low for 6 hours.

114. Hungarian Pea Stew

Servings: 8

Cooking Time: 6 hours

Ingredients

- 6 cups green peas
- 1-pound cubed pork

- 3 tablespoons olive oil
- 4 tablespoons almond flour
- 2 tablespoons minced parsley
- 1 cup water
- Salt to taste
- 1 cup coconut milk
- 1 teaspoon coconut sugar

Instructions

1.Put all ingredients in the slow cooker and cook on low for 6 hours.

115. A Simple Age-Old Bone Broth

Preparation Time: 10 minutes
Cooking Time: 75 minutes
Servings: 2
Ingredients:

- 1 cooked chicken carcass
- inch knob of ginger
- 1 chopped sized onion
- 1 cup of chopped up celery tops
- 2 tablespoon of apple cider vinegar
- 3 liters of water

Directions:

1. Add all of the listed ingredients to your pot. Pour 3 liters of water into the pot; cover and cook it for about 75 minutes on low heat. Stir frequently. Once done, turn off the heat, but don't remove the lid to release heat naturally. Allow it to cool down for about 1 hour.
2. Strain the solids into a large sized container and season the broth with some salt. Allow it to chill overnight. The day after, remove the solidified fat from the top. Divide it and enjoy!

116. Lamb and Vegetable Stew

Servings: 6
Cooking Time: 6 hours
Ingredients

- 2 pounds Lamb stew meat
- 2 chopped Tomatoes
- 1 Summer squash
- 1 Zucchini
- 1 cup Mushrooms, sliced
- 1/2 Bell peppers, chopped
- 1 Onions, chopped
- Salt
- 1 garlic clove, crushed
- 1/2 teaspoon Thyme leaves
- 4 Bay leaves
- 2 cups chicken broth

Instructions

1.Cut squash and zucchini. Place vegetables and lamb in crockpot. Mix salt, garlic, thyme, and bay leaf into broth and pour over lamb and vegetables. Cover and cook on low for 6 hours. Serve over brown rice.

117. Zucchini, Tomato & Pork Stew

Servings: 8
Cooking Time: 3 hours
Ingredients

- 2 cups cooked corn
- 1 chopped onion
- 2 sliced zucchinis
- 2 chopped tomato
- 2 tablespoon olive oil
- 2 garlic cloves
- Salt and pepper
- 4 pounds cubed pork

Instructions

1.Put ingredients in the pot. Cover, and cook on low for 3 hours.

118. Spinach Mushroom Soup

Preparation Time: 10 minutes

Cooking Time: 5 minutes

Servings: 3

Ingredients:

- 1 tablespoon olive oil
- 1 teaspoon garlic, chopped
- 1 cup spinach, torn
- ½ cup mushrooms, chopped
- Salt and pepper, to taste
- ½ teaspoon tamari
- 3 cups vegetable stock
- 1 teaspoon sesame seeds, roasted

Directions:

1. Heat on medium the olive oil in a skillet. Add garlic to the hot oil and sauté for 30 seconds or until fragrant. Add spinach and mushrooms, then sauté for 1 minute or until lightly tender.
2. Add salt, black pepper, tamari, and vegetable stock. Cook for another 3 minutes. Stir constantly.
3. Garnish with sesame seeds and serve warm.

119. Garlicky Chicken Soup

Preparation Time: 10 minutes

Cooking Time: 10 minutes

Servings: 4

Ingredients:

- 2 tablespoons butter
- 1 large chicken breast chopped
- 4 ounces cream cheese, cubed
- 2 tablespoons garlic powder
- ½ cup heavy cream
- 14½ ounces chicken broth
- Salt, to taste

Directions:

1. Place a skillet and add butter to melt on medium heat. Add chicken strips and sauté for 2 minutes. Add cream cheese and garlic powder, and cook for 3 minutes, stirring occasionally.
2. Pour in the heavy cream and chicken broth. Bring the soup to a boil, then lower the heat. Simmer the soup for 4 minutes, then sprinkle with salt. Let cool for 5 minutes and serve warm.

120. Lamb and Sweet Potato Stew

Servings: 8

Cooking Time: 6 hours

Ingredients

- 1 cup tomato paste
- 1/4 cup lemon juice
- 2 tablespoons mustard
- Salt and pepper to taste
- 1/2 cup soft almond butter
- 3 cubed sweet potatoes
- 1/2 garlic clove minced
- 4 pounds boneless chuck roast

Instructions

1.In a large bowl, combine tomato paste, lemon juice, almond butter and mustard. Stir in salt, pepper, garlic and cubed sweet potato. Place chuck roast in a slow cooker. Pour tomato mixture over chuck roast. Cover, and cook on low for 6 hours.

121. Cauliflower Curry Soup

Preparation Time: 15 minutes

Cooking Time: 26 minutes

Servings: 4

Ingredients:

- 2 tablespoons avocado oil
- 1 white onion, chopped

- 4 garlic cloves, chopped
- ½ Serrano pepper, chopped
- inch ginger, chopped
- ¼ teaspoon turmeric powder
- 2 teaspoons curry powder
- ½ teaspoon black pepper
- 1 teaspoon salt
- 1 cup of water
- 1 large cauliflower, cut into florets
- 1 cup chicken broth
- 1 can unsweetened coconut milk
- Cilantro, for garnish

Directions:

1. Place a saucepan over medium heat and add oil to heat. Add onions to the hot oil and sauté them for 3 minutes. Add garlic, Serrano pepper, and ginger, then sauté for 2 minutes.
2. Add turmeric, curry powder, black pepper, and salt. Cook for 1 minute after a gentle stir.
3. Pour water into the pan, then add cauliflower. Cover this soup with a lid and cook for 10 minutes. Stir constantly. Remove the soup from the heat and allow it to cool at room temperature. Transfer this soup to a blender and purée the soup until smooth.
4. Return the soup to the saucepan and add broth and coconut milk. Cook for 10 minutes more and stir frequently.
5. Divide the soup into four bowls and sprinkle the cilantro on top for garnish before serving.

122. Asparagus Cream Soup

Preparation Time: 15 minutes
Cooking Time: 22 minutes
Servings: 6
Ingredients:

- 4 tablespoons butter
- 1 small onion, chopped
- 6 cups low-sodium chicken broth
- Salt and pepper, to taste
- 2 pounds asparagus, cut in half
- ½ cup sour cream

Directions:

1. Place a large pot over low heat and add butter to melt. Add onion to the melted butter and sauté for 2 minutes or until soft. Add chicken broth, salt, black pepper, and asparagus. Bring the soup to a boil, then cover the lid and cook for 20 minutes. Remove the pot from the heat and allow it to cool for 5 minutes. Transfer the soup to a blender and blend until smooth. Add sour cream and pulse again to mix well. Serve fresh and warm.

123. Lamb Soup

Preparation Time: 10 minutes
Cooking Time: 4 hours
Servings: 4
Ingredients:

- ½ cup broccoli, chopped
- 7 oz lamb fillet, chopped
- ¼ teaspoon ground cumin
- ¼ daikon, chopped
- 2 bell peppers, chopped
- 1 tablespoon avocado oil
- 5 cups beef broth

Directions:

1. Add all ingredients to the pot and cook for 4 hours. Serve warm.

124. Basic Minestrone Soup

Preparation Time: 10 minutes

Cooking Time: 2 hours 30 minutes

Servings: 4

Ingredients:

- 1 ½ cup ground pork
- ½ bell pepper, chopped
- 2 tablespoons chives, chopped
- 2 oz celery stalk, chopped
- 1 teaspoon butter
- 1 teaspoon Italian seasonings
- 4 cups chicken broth
- ½ cup mushrooms, sliced

Directions:

1. Add all ingredients to the pot and cook for 2 hours 30 minutes. Serve warm.

125. Chorizo Soup

Preparation Time: 10 minutes

Cooking Time: 3 hours

Servings: 3 servings

Ingredients:

- 8 oz chorizo, chopped
- 1 teaspoon tomato paste
- 4 oz scallions, diced
- 1 tablespoon dried cilantro
- ½ teaspoon chili powder
- 1 teaspoon avocado oil
- 2 cups beef broth

Directions:

1. Add all ingredients to the pot and cook for 3 hours. Serve warm.

126. Red Feta Soup

Preparation Time: 10 minutes

Cooking Time: 1 hour 30 minutes

Servings: 4

Ingredients:

- 1 cup broccoli, chopped
- 1 teaspoon tomato paste
- ½ cup coconut cream
- 4 cups beef broth
- 1 teaspoon chili flakes
- 6 oz feta, crumbled

Directions:

1. Add all ingredients to the pot and cook for 1 hour 30 minutes. Serve warm.

127. "Ramen" Soup

Preparation Time: 10 minutes

Cooking Time: 1 hour 30 minutes

Servings: 2

Ingredients:

- 1 zucchini, trimmed
- 2 cups chicken broth
- 2 eggs, boiled, peeled
- 1 tablespoon coconut aminos
- 5 oz beef loin, strips
- 1 teaspoon chili flakes
- 1 tablespoon chives, chopped
- ½ teaspoon salt

Directions:

1. Add all ingredients to the pot and cook for 1 hour 30 minutes. Serve warm.

128. Tomatillos Fish Stew

Preparation Time: 15 minutes

Cooking Time: 1 hour 30 minutes

Servings: 2

Ingredients:

- 2 tomatillos, chopped
- 10 oz salmon fillet, chopped
- 1 teaspoon ground paprika
- ½ teaspoon ground turmeric

- 1 cup coconut cream
- ½ teaspoon salt

Directions:

1. Add all ingredients to the pot and cook for 1 hour 30 minutes. Serve warm.

129. Chili Verde Soup

Preparation Time: 10 minutes
Cooking Time: 2 hours
Servings: 4
Ingredients:

- 2 oz chili Verde sauce
- ½ cup Cheddar cheese, shredded
- 5 cups chicken broth
- 2 pounds chicken breast, boneless
- 1 tablespoon dried cilantro

Directions:

1. Add all ingredients to the pot and cook for 2 hours. Serve warm.

130. Steak Soup

Preparation Time: 10 minutes
Cooking Time: 4 hours
Servings: 5
Ingredients:

- 5 oz scallions, diced
- 1 tablespoon coconut oil
- 1 oz daikon, diced
- pound beef round steak, chopped
- 1 teaspoon dried thyme
- 5 cups of water
- ½ teaspoon ground black pepper

Directions:

1. Add all ingredients to the pot and cook for 4 hours. Serve warm.

131. Red Gazpacho Cream Soup

Preparation Time: 15 minutes
Cooking Time: 20 minutes
Servings: 10
Ingredients:

- 1 large red bell pepper, halved
- 1 large green bell pepper, halved
- 2 tablespoons basil, chopped
- 4 medium tomatoes
- 1 small red onion
- 1 large cucumber, diced
- 2 medium spring onions, diced
- 2 tablespoons apple cider vinegar
- 2 garlic cloves
- 2 tablespoons fresh lemon juice
- 1 cup extra virgin olive oil
- Salt and pepper, to taste
- 1¼ pounds feta cheese, shredded

Directions:

1. Preheat the oven to 400°F (205°C) and line a baking tray with parchment paper.
2. Place all the bell peppers in the baking tray and roast in the preheated oven for 20 minutes.
3. Remove the bell peppers from the oven. Allow to cool, then peel off their skin.
4. Transfer the peeled bell peppers to a blender along with basil, tomatoes, red onions, cucumber, spring onions, vinegar, garlic, lemon juice, olive oil, black pepper, and salt. Blend until the mixture smooth. Add black pepper and salt to taste. Garnish with feta cheese and serve warm.

132. Beef Taco Soup

Preparation Time: 15 minutes
Cooking Time: 24 minutes

Servings: 8

Ingredients:

- 2 garlic cloves, minced
- ½ cup onions, chopped
- pound (454 g) ground beef
- 1 teaspoon chili powder
- 1 tablespoon ground cumin
- 8-ounce cream cheese, softened
- 10-ounce diced tomatoes and green chilies
- ½ cup heavy cream
- 2 teaspoons salt
- 14½-ounce beef broth

Directions:

1. Take a large saucepan and place it over medium-high heat.
2. Add garlic, onions, and ground beef to the soup and sauté for 7 minutes until meat is browned.
3. Add chili powder and cumin, then cook for 2 minutes.
4. Add cream cheese and cook for 5 minutes while mashing the cream cheese into the beef with a spoon. Add diced tomatoes and green chilies, heavy cream, salt and broth then cook for 10 minutes. Mix gently and serve warm.

133. Creamy Tomato Soup

Preparation Time: 15 minutes

Cooking Time: 30 minutes

Servings: 4

Ingredients:

- 2 cups of water
- 4 cups tomato juice
- 3 tomatoes, peeled, seeded and diced
- 14 leaves fresh basil
- 2 tablespoons butter
- 1 cup heavy whipping cream
- Salt and pepper, to taste

Directions:

1. Take a suitable pot and place it over medium heat. Add water, tomato juice, and tomatoes, then simmer for 30 minutes. Transfer the soup to a blender, then add basil leaves. Blend the soup until smooth. Return this tomato soup to the cooking pot and place it over medium heat. Add butter, heavy cream, salt, and black pepper. Cook and mix until the butter melts.
2. Serve warm and fresh.

Desserts

134. Quick Strawberries with Crème

Preparation Time: 20 minutes
Cooking Time: 40 minutes
Servings: 5
Ingredients:
Directions:

- 1 tsp vanilla extract
- 2 cups sliced fresh strawberries
- ½ cup fresh coconut milk

1. First of all, put a whisk and a copper bowl in the freezer for about 30 to 35 minutes before cooking. Put strawberries and vanilla in a bowl and stir gently. Cover and put in the fridge for 35 minutes. Next, pour coconut milk into the copper bowl and whisk until thickens slightly.
2. Finally place strawberries in individual dishes and cover with the crème. Enjoy!

135. Delightful Banana Dessert

Preparation Time: 15 minutes
Cooking Time: 40 minutes
Servings: 2
Ingredients:

- 4 tbsps. pecans

- Freshly ground nutmeg
- 1.5 tsp pure vanilla extract
- ¼ tsp ground allspice
- ½ tsp ground ginger
- 2 large ripe bananas

Directions:

1. Cut bananas in half lengthwise. Meanwhile, mix vanilla, ginger, and allspice in a small jar and shake well. Brush the mixture over bananas and put them cut side down on wax paper. Leave in freezer for 35 minutes. Toast pecans and chop finely. Finally garnish bananas with the pecans and sprinkle with nutmeg.

136. Awesome Spiced Orange Glazed Ham

Preparation Time: 40 minutes
Cooking Time: 2 hours 10 minutes
Servings: 1 to 2
Ingredients:

- 10 pounds cooked raw ham
- 3 tablespoons maple syrup

FOR THE RUB:

- 2 teaspoons onion powder
- ½ teaspoon cayenne
- ½ teaspoon smoked paprika
- ½ teaspoon cinnamon
- ½ teaspoon ground cloves

- ½ teaspoon garlic powder

FOR THE GLAZE:

- ½ cup coconut aminos
- 1 teaspoon chili powder
- 2 ½ tablespoons maple syrup
- ½ teaspoon smoked paprika
- ½ teaspoon fish sauce
- 2 cups orange juice
- Zest of about ½ orange
- FOR GARNISH:
- 4 navel oranges, cut in half

Directions: Preheat oven to 320 °F.

1. Combine onion powder, garlic powder, smoked paprika, ground clove, cinnamon, and cayenne. Put the raw ham into a pan and cover with the maple syrup. Rub the spice mixture onto the ham, completely covering it and letting it get between the slices.

2. Cover the ham with foil, put into the oven and bake for about 1.5 hours. Then half an hour before the ham is done, add orange juice, coconut aminos, orange zest, maple syrup, fish sauce, smoked paprika and chili powder into a large pan and mix well. Cook over medium heat for about 25 minutes, stirring frequently. When it is reduced by 1/3 and begins to boil, remove from heat. Remove foil from the ham, when done, and glaze the entire ham with half of the prepare orange glaze. Stick a few toothpicks through the ham to prevent unfolding and put orange halve around. Next, put the ham back into the oven and cook properly for about 30 to 35 more minutes at 400°F. Remove and glaze with the rest of the orange glaze. Finally serve.

137. Elegant Chocolate Orange and Mint Chip Truffles

Preparation Time: 10 minutes
Cooking Time: 25 to 30 minutes
Servings: 1 dozen truffles
Ingredients:
BASE:

- 6.5 tbsps. coconut butter
- ½ tsp pure vanilla extract
- 4 tbsps. coconut oil
- 4 tbsps. almond butter

MINT CHIP FLAVOR:

- 1 tsp pure maple syrup

- 2.5 tsps. mint extract
- 1 tbsp cacao nibs

FOR THE COATING:

- 2 tbsps. cacao powder
- Chocolate orange flavor:
- 2 tsps. pure maple syrup
- 2.5 tbsps. cocoa powder
- Zest of one orange
- 2 tbsps. shredded coconut
- About 1.5 tsp orange zest

Directions:
1. First of all, put the coconut oil, pure vanilla extract, coconut and almond butter into a bowl, and stir until well combined. Split the base in half add ingredients for mint chip flavor to one half, and ingredients for chocolate orange flavor to another half. Stir both mixtures thoroughly.
2. Next, put both mixtures in the freezer for about 10 to 15 minutes.
3. Form 1-inch balls with your hands and roll each one in the coating for its flavor. Finally place the balls on a plate and put in the fridge until solid.

138. Rich Omelet Under Applesauce

Preparation Time: 15 minutes
Cooking Time: 30 minutes
Servings: 1 dozen truffles
Ingredients:

- ½ teaspoon dash vanilla
- 2-3 strawberries
- ½ teaspoon cinnamon
- 2 tablespoons applesauce
- 3-4 eggs

Directions:
1. First of all, if you don't have applesauce, take 1/2 apple,

remove the core and the skin, fine grate the rest to get the applesauce. Slice the strawberries.

2. Pre-heat the skillet over medium heat.

3. Break the eggs into the bowl, add cinnamon and vanilla, stir thoroughly. Then pour the mixture on the skillet, cook it properly for about 2 to 5 minutes till it mostly ready, toss it.

4. Cook it properly for about 2 minutes, transfer it on the plate. Finally distribute the applesauce over the half of the omelet, add strawberry, fold it with another half and cut into 2 portions.

139. Very Sensual Strawberry Cheesecake

Preparation Time: 10 minutes
Cooking Time: 20 minutes
Servings: 8
Ingredients:

- 2 ounces full fat cream cheese
- 2/3 cup of sugar substitute
- 1 teaspoon of vanilla extract
- 2 eggs at room temperature
- Handful of fresh strawberries
- Strawberry syrup for garnish

Directions:

- Take a Spring Form pan and grease it up properly. Take a mixer and blend your cream cheese until there are no lumps found in it. Add sugar, vanilla extract, to the cream cheese and blend it again. Add the eggs (one at a time) and keep beating the mixture.

- Cover the bottom sides of your pan tightly with one piece of foil. Pour the batter into your Spring Form Pan. Take a pan bigger and add the appropriate amount of water to ensure that the pan is filled by 1-inch. Put the Spring Form Pan into the pan full of water.

- Bake at 300°F for about 30 minutes. Bake other 30 minutes at 120°F.

- Remove the cake to allow it to reach a room temperature. Cover the cake with a plastic wrap and allow it to chill for 5-6 hours in fridge. Serve with your favorite garnish!

140. Titanic Apple Butter

Preparation Time: 15 minutes
Cooking Time: 8 hours
Servings: 10
Ingredients:

- 1 teaspoon allspice
- 1 cup maple syrup
- 1.5 teaspoon clove
- 1/4 teaspoon nutmeg
- 1 teaspoon ginger powder
- 1 and 1/2 cups water
- 3 pounds apples, peeled
- 1.5 tablespoon cinnamon
- Juice of 1 lemon

Directions:

1. In your pot, mix apples with water, lemon juice, allspice, cinnamon, clove, ginger powder, maple syrup and nutmeg. Cover and cook properly on low heat for about 7 to 8 hours. Stir frequently. Then leave your mix to cool down for about 10 to 15 minutes, blend using an immersion blender and pour into small jars. Serve (also for garnish).

141. Unique Banana Pancakes

Preparation Time: 5 to 10 Minutes
Cooking Time: 15 minutes
Servings: 2 to 4
Ingredients:

- Vanilla Extract, dash (Optional)
- 1 free-range egg
- About 1.5 tsp cinnamon
- 1 tsp of coconut (Shredded)

- 1 banana (Mashed)
- Seeds for garnish (Optional)

Directions:

1. Mash one whole banana and lightly beat with an egg.
2. For extra flavor, add coconut chips, vanilla extract (just a dash) and cinnamon. Put this in a pan with a bit of oil on the bottom (or pour this mixture into a frying pan, if you have) and cook properly as you would a regular pancake.
3. Serve with garnish. Enjoy!

142. Awesome Safe Blueberry Muffin

Preparation Time: 15 Minutes
Cooking Time: 25 minutes
Servings: 2 to 4
Ingredients:

- 1 teaspoon coconut flour
- 3 tablespoons cinnamon
- ½ teaspoon baking soda
- 3/4 cup fresh blueberries
- 1/4 teaspoon salt
- 1/2 tablespoon vanilla
- 2 eggs
- 1/4 cup coconut oil
- 1/2 cup maple syrup
- 2 cups almond flour
- 1/3 cup coconut milk

Directions:

1. Preheat the oven to 350° F. Line a muffin tin and oil it up with coconut oil.
2. Combine flours, salt, and baking soda in a mixing bowl. Pour in eggs, maple syrup, coconut oil, coconut milk, and vanilla; then mix well. Gently fold in the blueberries and cinnamon, careful not to fold the mixture more than 10 times. Pour into muffin tin and sprinkle with extra cinnamon. Finally bake for about 20 to 25 minutes before allowing to cool. Then, enjoy!

143. Charming Blueberry lemon muffins

Preparation Time: 20 minutes
Cooking Time: 40 minutes
Servings: 12
Ingredients:

- ½ cup coconut oil
- 1 cup fresh blueberries
- ½ tsp pure vanilla extract
- ¼ tsp baking soda
- ¼ cup grade B maple syrup
- About 1 tsp salt
- 1 lemon, juice and zest
- ½ cup flour
- 6 eggs

Directions:

1. First of all, melt coconut oil. Next, mix the eggs, maple syrup, pure vanilla extract, lemon juice, and lemon zest and melted coconut oil. Sift in the salt, flour, and baking soda, and blend until smooth. Add the blueberries. Stir properly. Fill 3/4 of the batter into the baking silicon cups.

2. Finally bake for about 35 to 40 minutes to 350°F. Serve.

144. Wonderful Sweet potato pancakes

Preparation Time: 20 minutes
Cooking Time: 20 minutes
Servings: 4
Ingredients:

- 3 eggs

- Pinch salt
- 15ml coconut oil
- 1/2 teaspoon rosemary
- 2 teaspoons coconut flour
- 5 sweet potatoes

Directions:

1. First of all, wash sweet potatoes, dry them with paper towels. Chop finely.
2. Pre-heat the skillet over medium-low heat, pout coconut oil.
3. Beat eggs in a mixing bowl with coconut flour, rosemary and salt. Add chopped sweet potatoes and mix thoroughly. Next, put the spoonful of the mixture on the skillet, cook properly for about 2 to 5 minutes on one side, toss and cook properly 2 more minutes.
4. Do it until there is no mixture left. Finally put the pancakes on the plate. Serve with garnish.

145. Elegant Shrimp Avocado Salad

Preparation Time: 5 minutes
Cooking Time: 5 minutes
Servings: 6
Ingredients:

- Pinch salt and pepper
- 100g cherry tomatoes
- 1/2 onion
- Pinch oregano
- 60ml olive oil

- 4 tbsps. chopped cilantro
- 2.5 teaspoons hot sauce
- 2 avocados
- 2 oranges
- 4 tablespoons lime juice
- 2.5 tablespoons chopped mint
- 2 tablespoons cooking fat
- 24 colossal shrimps

Directions:

1. Pre-heat a grill pan over high heat, add cooking fat.
2. Wash shrimps, then peel them off and devein. Mix olive oil, lime juice, hot sauce and mint in the bowl. Plunge shrimps in the mixture and place them on the grill pan. Fry for about 2 to 5 minutes on each side. Meanwhile wash avocados, oranges and tomatoes, dry them with paper towels. Cut tomatoes into halves, avocados into wedges and oranges into segments. Slice the onion and put it in the bowl with mixture together with oranges, tomatoes, avocados, cilantro and oregano. Mix well and put in the plates. Finally add grilled shrimps to the plates.

146. Rich Simple Breakfast Meatloaf

Preparation Time: 15 minutes
Cooking Time: 3 hours 20 minutes
Servings: 4 to 6
Ingredients:

- 2 pounds pork, minced
- 2 eggs

- 1.5 teaspoon red pepper flakes
- 1 teaspoon marjoram, dried
- 1 teaspoon coconut oil
- 1 tablespoon paprika
- 3 garlic cloves (Minced)
- 1/4 cup almond flour

- A pinch of sea salt
- 1.5 teaspoon oregano, minced
- 1 tablespoon sage, minced
- 1 onion, chopped

Directions:

1. First of all, heat up a pan with the oil over medium high heat, add onion, stir and cook properly for about 2 to 5 minutes. Add garlic, stir, cook properly for about 2 to 5 minutes more, take off heat and leave aside to cool down.
2. In a bowl, mix pork with a pinch of salt, pepper flakes, flour, paprika, oregano, sage, marjoram and eggs and whisk everything. Next, add garlic and onion and stir again. Shape your meatloaf, transfer to your pot, cover and cook properly on low for about 3.5 hours. Stir frequently.
3. Finally leave aside to cool down, slice and serve.

147. Titanic Paleo Strawberry Clementine Smoothie

Preparation Time: 10 minutes
Cooking Time: 0 minutes
Servings: 2
Ingredients:

- 1.5 banana, frozen, chopped into chunks
- 8 oozes strawberries – frozen or fresh
- 2 Clementines or Mandarins

Directions:

1. First of all, thaw the frozen banana chunks for at least 5 to 10 minutes.
2. Slightly defrost the frozen strawberries; then in the meantime, peel clementines and remove seeds. Finally combine all the ingredients in a blender and pulse until very smooth.
3. Put the mix in a cup and serve with garnish if you want.

148. Tasty Paleo Breakfast Burrito

Preparation Time: 5 to 10 minutes
Cooking Time: 5 to 10 minutes
Servings: 1 to 3
Ingredients:

- Eggs – 2
- Salsa guacamole (optional)
- Chopped vegetables
- 1 cup spinach,
- 4 black olives,
- 1 bell pepper, chopped
- 1 tomato, chopped
- Sliced meat fat - 2

Directions:

1. Over medium heat, sauté the veggies in a bit of oil for about 2 to 5 minutes.
2. Meanwhile, in a bowl whisk the eggs then pour the mixed vegetables. Use a spatula to scramble the mixture until cooked through. Remove the eggs from the pan then have them rolled around the fat slices; then return them back to the skillet. Grill for about 30 to 40 seconds or until the fat slices turns slightly brown. Finally, you can serve it with guacamole, salsa or fresh cilantro topping.

149. Vintage Canned Tuna Ceviche

Preparation Time: 20 minutes
Cooking Time: 0 minutes
Servings: 2
Ingredients:

- Limes – 2
- Sliced avocado – 2
- Salt and pepper as needed
- Tabasco sauce – 3 drops
- Olive oil – 1.5 tsp.

- 7 oz. tuna packed in water, drained
- Jalapeno – 1, minced
- Seeded plum tomato – 1, diced
- Chopped cilantro – 2.5 tbsps.
- Minced red onion – 2 tbsps.

Directions:
1. First of all, in a bowl, combine olive oil, juice of 1 lime, a pinch of kosher salt and red onion.
2. Mix in the tabasco, jalapeno, tomato, drained tuna, and chopped cilantro. Taste and adjust seasoning, then cover and marinate in the refrigerator for minimum 20 to 25 minutes.
3. Finally, top with fresh sliced avocado and serve.

150. Best Chicken with Mushroom Sauce

Preparation Time: 15 minutes
Cooking Time: 20 minutes
Servings: 4
Ingredients:
- 4.5 teaspoons olive oil
- ¼ cup chopped parsley
- 3 cloves garlic minced
- Salt and pepper to taste
- 12 ounces sliced mushrooms
- 1 cup fat free chicken broth
- 8 chicken tenderloins

Directions:
1. Preheat oven to 200°F. Sprinkle the chicken with salt and pepper.
2. Slice garlic and mushrooms. Add olive oil to a large skillet and heat over medium heat.
3. Add chicken and cook properly for about 5 to 10 minutes per side; then transfer to the oven.
4. Next, please add a little more oil to the skillet and then cook garlic for a few seconds before adding the mushrooms. Sprinkle the mushrooms with salt and pepper and cook, stirring once in a while, for about 5 to 10 minutes, until golden. Meanwhile, chop the parsley. Pour in chicken broth and stir in parsley, at the same time removing any brown bits from the bottom. Cook until the broth is reduced in half. Serve the chicken topped with mushroom sauce.

151. Nostalgic Lemon Poppyseed Mini Muffins

Preparation Time: 10 minutes
Cooking Time: 20 minutes
Servings: 5
Ingredients:
- 1 teaspoon baking soda
- 1 tablespoon water
- ¼ teaspoon organic sweetener
- ¼ cup lemon juice, + 1 tablespoon
- 2 tablespoons poppy seeds
- ¼ teaspoon salt
- 3 eggs
- 1.5 tablespoon raw honey
- 1 large lemon, zested
- 1/2 cup coconut flour
- 2.5 tablespoons butter, melted

Directions:
1. Preheat oven to 350° F. Oil the mini muffin pan with coconut oil or use liners.
2. In a bowl, add the dry ingredients and mix. Then, quickly add the remaining ingredients except the water and then mix until batter is wet and well incorporated. Let the batter sit once becoming foamy and thick for about 2 to 5 minutes. Add the water and blend again.
3. Scoop the batter into the muffin pan and bake for about 10 to 15 minutes. Finally cool a rack, and then enjoy!

152. Mighty Paleo Crock Pot Beef Stew

Preparation Time: 30 minutes
Cooking Time: 6 hours 10 minutes
Servings: 6
Ingredients:

- 3 carrots, chopped
- Salt and pepper, each
- 1 cup peas, frozen
- 1 bay leaf
- 2 celery stalks, chopped
- 1.5 tablespoon tapioca flour
- 1 teaspoon thyme
- 1 large onion, chopped
- 2 garlic cloves, minced
- 3 cups beef broth
- 1.5 teaspoon parsley
- 1 cup chopped mushrooms
- 2 tablespoons tomato paste
- 1 tablespoon paprika
- 2 pounds ground chuck, boneless
- 1 Tablespoon garlic powder

Directions:

1. Add the meat, vegetables and flour to the pot. Stir together to coat ingredients. Stir in the onion, celery, garlic cloves, peas and seasoning. Add the broth, tomato paste. Stir well. Cover and cook properly on low for approximately 7 to 8 hours. Stir occasionally. If the mixture seems dry, quickly add more broth. Take out the bay leaf. Finally serve in bowls.

153. King sized Cherry-Berry Medley

Preparation Time: 20 minutes
Cooking Time: 40 minutes
Servings: 4
Ingredients:

- 1/2 cup blueberries
- 4 chopped mint leaves
- ½ cup golden raspberries
- ½ tsp ground cinnamon
- ½ cup blackberries
- 1 tsp clove powder
- 1 tsp vanilla extract
- 1/2 cup bing/rainier cherries

Directions:

1. Pit and chop the cherries. Combine all the berries in a bowl, add spices and chopped mint and toss gently; then chill for about 30 to 35 minutes. Garnish with mint leaves and serve

154. Perfect Berry Delicious Smoothie

Preparation Time: 15 minutes
Cooking Time: 0 minutes
Servings: 3
Ingredients:

- Drop vanilla essence
- 2 cups mixed frozen berries
- 10 ice cubes
- 210 ml coconut Water

Directions:

1. Blend together all ingredients in a blender until very smooth. Finally add a little coconut milk if you like the smoothie to be thick. Enjoy!

155. Dashing Mini Baked Sweet Potato

Preparation Time: 5 minutes
Cooking Time: 10 minutes
Servings: 4
Ingredients:

- Chopped chives – 4 teaspoons
- Olive oil – 1.5 teaspoon
- Salt – ½ teaspoon
- Water – 1 cup
- Sweet potatoes – 4

Directions:

1. Prick the sweet potatoes using a fork then rub them with oil. Put the potatoes in a pot full of water and cook them for about 25 minutes; alternatively, if you have it, add water into the potatoes then place in microwave and cook at high heat for about 10 to 15 minutes. Cool them slightly once cooked. Split the potatoes partially into half lengthwise then fluff using a fork.

2. Finally sprinkle with salt and top with chives.

Bibliography

From the same author:

EASY ONE-POT PALEO COOKBOOK: Fast and Easy Meals for your busy LIFE: More than 250 Healthy Paleo Recipes and a 28-Day Meal Plan to organize your busy cooking!

EASY ONE-POT PALEO COOKBOOK: Easy Meals for your busy COOKING: 150+ Healthy Paleo Recipes to cook dirtying very little!

EASY ONE-POT PALEO COOKBOOK: Easy Meals for your Paleo DIET: 100+ Healthy Recipes to cook dirtying very little!

Conclusion

Thank you for reading this book!

I hope this book will help you deal with the lack of time in the busy modern world. Your family will be satisfied, you will consume healthy food, and have more time to do the things that you want.

I hope this is not only a usual cookbook that you will forget about after a short time, but a guide allows you to have healthier and more time for yourself! **Enjoy your delicious meals!**

Thanks very much for reading, and I wish you to achieve all your goals!

Clarissa Williams

CPSIA information can be obtained
at www.ICGtesting.com
Printed in the USA
BVHW052334010621
608544BV00009B/2896